Landscaping With Trees & Shrubs

Published by Linden Hills Press

Trade distribution by Voyageur Press
P.O. Box 338
Stillwater, MN 55082

Page Layout and Assembly by Anderberg-Lund Printing Company
Printed and bound in the United States by
Anderberg-Lund Printing Company

ISBN 0-9628378-2-2

Acknowledgement

The publisher is grateful to the following persons for their continued support of this series: Dorothy Johnson for her help even while planning the move into the new MSHS building, Jodi Lind-Hohman for her illustrations and plant knowledge, Jack Anderberg for contributing his resources, and all the contributors to the *Minnesota Horticulturist* for their love of gardening and the ability and desire to share their love and knowledge of gardening with the rest of us.

Thank you,
David Hohman
Publisher

Photo Credits

Cover - MSHS; page 4 - Ray; page 8 - D. Emerson; page 26 - MSHS; page 44 - MSHS; page 60 - C. King; page 78 - MSHS.

Table of Contents

Chapter 1: Planning and Design

Chapter 2: Landscaping With Trees

Chapter 3: Landscaping With Shrubs

Chapter 4: Landscaping for Special Interest

Chapter 5: Care and Maintenance

Zone Map

About the Authors

Foreword

The Northern Gardener's Library is based upon articles originally published in *Minnesota Horticulturist* magazine. Trusted as a reliable resource to northern horticulture for more than 100 years, *Minnesota Horticulturist* is the oldest continuously-published periodical in Minnesota. The official publication of the Minnesota State Horticultural Society (MSHS), *Minnesota Horticulturist* began relating experiences of horticulturists who moved to Minnesota to help feed the growing population. These pioneers faced unexpected challenges attempting to grow the fruits and vegetables they brought from Europe and the Eastern United States.

Minnesota Horticulturist has evolved to meet the needs of amateur horticulturists – gardeners who enjoy their hobby within small or large home grounds. Writers share their own experiences, which bring research and experimentation to a practical level in the home garden.

This book shares the experience of seasoned gardeners, many of whom write regularly for *Minnesota Horticulturist*. Their practical advice is based upon observations, trials and successes. Care has been taken to explain environmentally-conscious techniques and growing practices.

Two volumes in the Northern Gardener's Library series are being published in 1992: *Container Gardening* and *Landscaping with Trees & Shrubs*. The first two volumes were published in 1991: *The Good Gardener* and *Flower Gardens*. Future volumes will feature other popular horticultural themes.

All volumes in the series concentrate on the unique needs and challenges of growing home gardens in the lovely, but often harsh, climates of the northern states and Canada. Written for hardiness Zones 3 and 4, the information on culture and varieties is also valuable for Zone 5 gardens.

Introduction

To improve the liveability of your yard, plan outdoor living spaces to meet your family's needs and include plenty of trees and shrubs. These dependable, permanent garden features help define your space, to create privacy or frame a pleasing view.

Northern gardeners have shared their best ideas and methods on hardy trees and shrubs in *Landscaping with Trees and Shrubs*. Learn about special interest landscapes, including use of native plants, plants to attract birds and butterflies, fall color, and more. Turn your shady spot into a jewel using plants which will thrive in low-light conditions. Read about trees especially developed for smaller city lots, and diverse woody plants to meet the needs of the largest acreage. Expand your knowledge of plant material choices.

All seasons are important in the northern garden. Learn to recognize how permanent plantings enhance the home landscape throughout the year through unique form, shape and color.

In harsh northern climates, choosing dependably hardy plant materials makes the difference between success and failure. Planting and maintenance techniques are also important. The northern gardeners who write for *Minnesota Horticulturist* are here to assist you in *Landscaping with Trees & Shrubs*.

Dorothy B. Johnson
Executive Director
Minnesota State Horticultural Society

Chapter 1

Planning and Design

Choosing Landscape Evergreens

Planning Tips and Design Goals

Planting Considerations

Planting Trees for
Energy Conservation

Mapping Your Home Landscape

Choosing Landscape Evergreens

Jane P. McKinnon

lanting and caring for evergreens requires a considerable investment of time and money, so it is important to make the right decisions when selecting landscape evergreens.

To choose wisely, you need two kinds of information. First, you need to know about each plant's size at maturity, shape, and year-round appearance to decide whether the plant will serve your purpose. Second, you must be sure that any species or variety you consider can grow vigorously in the climate and site conditions of the property you intend to develop. This chapter will provide guidelines to help you select evergreen trees and shrubs for cold-climate landscaping.

Learning about the habits and needs of evergreens is worth the effort. Nursery-grown evergreens of landscape grade are expensive. Years of care are required to produce well-shaped tops and ample root systems restricted enough for easy transplanting, whether balled and burlapped or container-grown. More years of care are required to develop evergreens to mature beauty in a new site. If you make the right choice at the beginning, not only will you save time and money, but your landscape evergreens will serve a useful purpose, be it to provide year-long beauty or to give shelter.

Evergreens As Design Materials

An obvious consideration in choosing evergreens is how they will look in the landscape. You need to take into account each plant's size at maturity, shape, color, texture, and contribution to a harmonious landscape design.

Size Most Minnesotans admire and appreciate native evergreens in the state's forested lands. Pine, spruce, fir, and arborvitae, whether frosted with snow or tipped with new spring growth, symbolize the beauty of the north. As many vacationers may remember, these native species can be enormous trees at maturity. When spruce, fir, or arborvitae are grown in unrestricted spaces, they cover a wider and wider circle over the ground as they develop, often reaching 30 feet across. Pines are also cone-shaped as young trees, but as they mature to an irregular shape they often lose lower branches, leaving open space beneath. They can reach 50 feet or more in height and their roots fill a large circle of soil under their foliage, making it difficult to grow turf and other plants. Most home properties have limited space for evergreen trees 40 to 50 feet high, occupying 30 feet at the base. One large evergreen tree with thick foliage touching the ground can shelter the northwest exposure of most town or suburban home properties, but it may be too large for a city lot. Where a group of evergreen trees might seem more

This evergreen needs more space to grow properly. (Hohman)

effective than just one tree, a good choice would be the smaller upright junipers or columnar arborvitae because they are often more in scale with residential sites. These evergreens will mature at 20 to 30 feet, with a spread of 5 to 10 feet depending on the variety.

Evergreen shrubs also require careful spacing, especially since they are so often planted at doorways or at the base or foundation of a house. Juniper shrubs with horizontal shapes can spread to five or six feet in a few years; heights vary considerably according to the cultivar (cultivated variety). An 18-inch high Skandia juniper is far more useful under a ground-level window than its 5-foot relative, Savin juniper. Japanese yew are often pruned tightly to keep them at a desired height or width, but some selections will grow into 20-foot trees or very wide shrubs over time.

It is important to remember that plants for sale in nurseries are young enough and small enough to handle and are offered at a price customers will pay. Differences in these evergreens are not apparent to customers unfamiliar with variety names. Do not make the mistake of expecting welch juniper or pyramid arborvitae to remain the dwarf shrubs they appear to be in the nursery sales lot. Check the catalogs, ask for fact sheets at your county extension office, consult with experienced nursery people, and study plantings in your own community. You need to know which tree or shrub best fits the space you want to fill with evergreen foliage.

Shape Evergreen trees and shrubs are conspicuous and dominant in landscape designs because of their strong shapes, dense foliage, and dark, heavy effect. These qualities influence the way people respond to spaces landscaped with evergreens. Crowded, upright forms blocking windows can smother a building with oppressive foliage. Too many evergreens can make an outdoor space gloomy and depressing. On the

These north-facing evergreens help protect and frame this house. (MSHS)

other hand, a south-facing mass of pines can form a winter suntrap, reflecting light and pleasant warmth to a driveway, walk, or house beyond. The strong outline of a columnar evergreen can call attention to a view or emphasize a pathway. But such an exclamation point is not suitable for framing a garage door or calling attention to a power pole. A soft, horizontal line of spreading junipers or yews without any distraction of varying shapes or sizes can be a satisfying transition from house wall to ground level.

Color and texture The different colors and textures of foliage, bark, cones, or berries should also be considered in selecting evergreens. There are silvery-blue juniper varieties (trees, shrubs, or ground covers) that are often effective as a contrast to redwood surfaces. Dark green Japanese yew, with the female plants bearing red berries in fall and winter, are handsome against many colors of brick. Scotch pine's cinnamon orange bark and bluish green needles are prettier in winter than the purplish brown Eastern redcedars. Deep green spruce or balsam fir contrasted with red maples present a pleasing scene.

But color and texture variations must be carefully used. Soft foliaged yellow-green arborvitae do not blend well with stiff Colorado blue spruce. Any closely planted

These textures and colors create a harmonious scene. (MSHS)

mixture of textures and shades of green will appear not as a harmonious group but as a crowded collection of individual trees. Plant conspicuous evergreens only occasionally, when an eye-catching specimen is particularly needed.

Landscape design Landscape plantings, whether for home properties or large public grounds, are most satisfying when a clear pattern is apparent to people using the space. Simplicity and serenity are important for outdoor design. Use the fewest possible variety of evergreen plants and select them for an obvious purpose. For example, you may want them to provide four-season beauty and year-round privacy for outdoor living spaces or views from windows and glass walls. Or you may need protection from the elements. Massed evergreens block noise and provide shelter for people, buildings, gardens, and wildlife against strong winds and driving snow. Evergreen windbreaks and shelterbelts have long been used for midwestern farmsteads, with resulting higher winter temperatures, lower wind velocities, and more convenient snow accumulations. Old, mature pines can broaden to furnish shade, and their needles underfoot provide a quiet and soft surface. Large spruce and fir can be dramatic specimens in park-like spaces. Closely planted upright junipers or arborvitae can be impenetrable hedges, either for protection against trespassers or as a background and windscreen for flowers. Dwarf evergreens can give stability and substance to rock gardens, borders, and entrance plantings where strong shapes and year-round foliage are needed to complement softer flowers and deciduous shrubs.

Climate And Site Requirements

Cold hardiness is the first test a plant must pass to be considered suitable for Minnesota landscaping. The USDA plant hardiness map is a standard reference for approximate ranges of average annual minimum temperatures. Minnesota is divided roughly in half between Zones 3 and 4, with a strip of Zone 4's milder temperatures along the shores of Lake Superior. You can see from the map (page 95) that the northern United States is not all in the same zone. The climate of the Pacific northwest or New England, for instance, is modified by ocean currents and mountain ranges, whereas Minnesota is exposed to winter blasts of Arctic air. Many plants listed in nursery catalogs as suitable for other states bordering Canada do not survive in Minnesota. Reputable mail-order nursery firms identify zones of cold hardiness in their catalogs, and experienced Minnesota nursery people can offer firsthand information on winter survival of evergreen plants.

But the large-scale temperature zone divisions are sometimes not precise enough for choosing evergreens for long life and vigor. Plants may grow well in extreme southern Minnesota and freeze out in Minneapolis, although both are in Zone 4. Evergreens exposed to wind on hilltops or on the western sides and corners of buildings are stressed both by cold and drought. Plants in a sheltered setting may grow in localities outside their normal hardiness zone, but an extremely cold winter may remove

such exotics from the landscape. The term "microclimate" is used to describe these smaller-scaled differences in growing conditions. Thus, using a hardy plant such as mugo pine or savin juniper in an exposed location is safer than planting a less tolerant species. Black Hills spruce will grow well in colder, dryer locations, but white fir needs a moist, rich soil and milder temperatures. These differences may be important when choosing a specimen evergreen tree for your property.

In addition to survival, resistance to injury is another cold hardiness requirement for evergreens in a landscape. Tip-kill (dieback of upper shoots and branch ends) and winter burn (browning of foliage) are symptoms of winter damage. Although the plants live, they are disfigured until pruning and new growth can improve their appearance. During some winters, evergreens are damaged by fluctuations in temperature that cannot be prevented, but planting evergreens in locations exposed to the warmth of the afternoon sun on bright winter days is not prudent. When the sun goes down, or moves behind an obstruction, the plant may suddenly be plunged into sub-zero cold, with resulting damage. If an evergreen is needed in such an exposed place, check with local nurseries and observe successful plantings in your own community before choosing a variety. Maney juniper, for instance, seems to be more resistant to winter burn than Pfitzer juniper or Japanese yew. Welch juniper is usually less affected by tip-kill than Spiny Greek or Irish juniper, both sometimes attempted in Minnesota.

Soil and moisture requirements of evergreens hardy in Minnesota vary enough to allow selections for many different site conditions. Available moisture is as important as temperature for plant hardiness. Well-watered evergreens often survive when other plants fail, but those struggling through a dry summer in weakened condition are often dead after a cold winter. Dwarf junipers and Japanese yew in foundation plantings close to house walls, or overhung by wide eaves, often die from the combination of drought and cold.

More rainfall and snowmelt usually occurs in eastern Minnesota than in the west, but within each area there are soils that differ in their ability to hold moisture for plant growth. Sandy soils are droughty, while silts and clays may be so poorly drained that some plant roots lack sufficient oxygen. Well-drained loams are ideal for most evergreens, but pines and junipers are more tolerant of sandy, dry conditions than spruce, fir, and arborvitae. Heavy, well-drained soils grow magnificent white fir in Worthington, and Colorado spruce in Slayton, both

cities in southwestern Minnesota. Arborvitae and black spruce will grow in the wet soils of ditch banks, low-lying spots, pond edges, and lake shores, where other evergreens fail. Balsam fir grows well in locations that are damp for part of the year.

Most Minnesota soils are fertile and acid enough for evergreens suited to existing temperature and moisture conditions. However, soils of western Minnesota, and other places where limestone is the underlying rock, may have a high pH. This condition may cause a tie-up of soil iron, stunting the plant and yellowing the foliage. Arborvitae, junipers, Ponderosa pine, and white and Colorado spruce are generally tolerant of the higher pH soils in Minnesota.

One way to improve your chances of growing healthy evergreens even without an ideal microclimate is to copy forest conditions. Evergreens in nature are mulched by their own fallen needles and other forest litter. Soils are usually moist, modified with rotting organic matter, and protected against sudden temperature changes. If your landscape design can include mulched planting areas to improve soil-moisture relationships and prevent competition from weeds and grass, your evergreens will grow better. Extra watering will still be needed in dry weeks during the growing season, but plants will not be stressed as much as those growing over bare ground or mowed lawn.

Light requirements for healthy evergreen growth must be accommodated by selecting the appropriate plant for each location. Canada hemlock, Japanese yew, and Canada yew will grow in shade in Minnesota. However, Canada hemlock requires shelter from wind and a moist soil. Canada yew is not usually available in commercial nurseries. Several successful cultivars of Japanese yew are offered by Minnesota nurseries, but moisture and protection from winter sun are usually advised for these plants. American arborvitae varieties will tolerate partial shade, but develop more vigorously in open sunlight. They may need early replacement if grown in dark places. If other conditions are suitable, balsam fir, white pine, and douglas fir will grow where light may be filtered for part of the day. Junipers, spruce, and all other pines need full sunlight. Shape, growth rate, color, and pest tolerance are all diminished by planting these species under other trees or in the shadow of buildings.

Evergreens for Problem Sites

Site Condition	Recommended Evergreens
Clay Soil	Arborvitae, Austrian Pine, Ponderosa Pine, White Fir, Colorado Spruce
Sandy Soil	Jack Pine, Mugo Pine, Norway Pine, Scotch Pine
Wet Soil	American Arborvitae, Balsam Fir, Black Spruce
High pH	Arborvitae, Black Hills Spruce, Colorado Spruce, Mugo Pine, Ponderosa Pine, Junipers
Windy/exposed	Black Hills Spruce, Jack Pine, Mugo Pine, Ponderosa Pine, Rocky Mountain Juniper, Savin Juniper, Eastern Redcedar
Partial Sun	Arborvitae, Balsam Fir, Douglas Fir
Shade	Canada Hemlock, Canada Yew, Japanese Yew

Planning Tips and Design Goals

Dorothy Johnson

Does your outdoor living space meet the needs of your family? A yard of any size can serve several outdoor living purposes. When beginning an improved landscape plan, envision the use and expectations for the outdoor space. Consider what your family's need for privacy is. Do you want to devote an area to food gardening or a water feature? Initial planning is a must to get the most from your yard - to develop a garden to fit your lifestyle.

OVERALL PLANNING CONSIDERATIONS:

☐ What are my priorities for my yard?

☐ What do family members currently use the space for; what changes do they want?

☐ Have changes of growing conditions (shade of sun, drainage, etc.) hampered the health or growth of present plant materials? And do I need major renovation, change of location, or different plant mixture to match changed growing conditions?

☐ Is gardening my passion or an incidental hobby?

USE TREES & SHRUBS TO DEVELOP PLEASING VIEWS

☐ Create an enclosed feeling with a background.

☐ Provide a shield for privacy from neighbors' yards or to focus a view onto an adjacent property.

☐ Offer a focal point or special view from outside or from inside windows where family and visitors usually view the yard.

☐ Improve winter vistas.

☐ Screen utility areas, kennel, driveway, or buildings.

USE TREES & SHRUBS TO ENHANCE OR DEVELOP LANDSCAPE FEATURES

☐ Attract birds, butterflies, and other wildlife with flowering and fruiting plantings.

☐ Create a pleasing variety of color, texture, and size.

☐ Protect your house from winter winds and summer heat.

☐ Define a private "secret" garden.

☐ Create outdoor "garden rooms" for orchards, lawn, play space, dining area, flower and vegetable gardens.

☐ Plant to enhance current features.

☐ Use a specimen plant as a focal point.

☐ Plan complimentary shrubs to enhance patio or deck.

CONSIDER MAINTENANCE NEEDS FOR EXISTING AND NEW PLANTS

☐ Is low maintenance a priority?

☐ If large trees are already on the site, check on their condition. Do they need pruning? Are they healthy?

☐ Learn how mulches keep soil cool, conserve moisture, and hamper weed growth.

☐ Make a yearly maintenance plan for watering, fertilizing, pruning, and other basics.

☐ To enhance long-term plant health, add soil amendments to planting areas.

Planting Considerations

After you have decided on your design goals, there are many practical considerations that you should take into account before making your final plant selections. They are:

Height - What is the ultimate height? Make sure you design with the mature size of the tree in mind. Always double check to make sure you have adequate clearance overhead from eaves or power lines.

Width - Always take into account the mature spread of the tree or shrub. Do not crowd!

Color - What kind of color are you looking for? Are you looking for early-season blossoms, a colorful leaf change in the fall, or the steady color of the evergreens?

Form and habit - What kind of maintenance requirements are there? Are you looking for a more formal look or less formal? Do the shrubs require regular pruning to look their best?

Sun - What kind of sun coverage do you get in the different areas of your yard? Are you planting under the dense canopy of a mature maple or in the filtered light next to a birch clump? Sun conditions may dictate what choice you have available to you.

Soil requirements - What kind of soil are you planning to plant in? Is it sandy, clayey, low pH or high pH? Some trees and shrubs are better suited for some soil conditions than others.

Fruit or Berries - Does the tree or shrub drop its fruit or retain them until eaten by birds? Are the berries attractive? Messy?

Hardiness - Are your selections appropriate for your area? Remember to take into account the microclimate of your yard. A marginally hardy shrub may survive in a sheltered area while a hardier shrub may not do well in a more exposed place in your yard.

Planting Trees for Energy Conservation

Peggy Sand

e have been hearing a lot of discussion lately about how trees can reduce our energy bills and rescue us from global warming. Among the figures that have received national and local attention are those stating that trees planted for energy conservation will save us 30 percent on cooling bills and 15 percent on heating bills. While there is good scientific evidence to support these numbers, it is important to understand how these figures and ideas apply under conditions in the Upper Midwest.

How Trees Affect the Environment

Trees and shrubs provide many benefits to our lives, including beauty, wildlife habitat, and increased property values. What is not as commonly known is that trees and shrubs can also save money and help the environment. Trees, and other vegetation, shelter buildings and modify local climate, effectively reducing the amount of fuel needed to heat and cool buildings.

From an energy conservation viewpoint, trees impact their environment in three basic ways. First, they block solar radiation. Typically we think of this as the shade they provide: the way they prevent the sun's rays and its heat from glaring in picture windows, from cooking air-conditioning units, and from baking the insides of cars. Trees in leaf can block 70 to 90 percent of solar radiation on clear days in summer. However, these same deciduous trees also have a significant shading impact in the winter. The branches and twigs of bare trees block 20 to 55 percent of the solar gain which is so beneficial in the winter.

Second, trees reduce wind speed, gently filtering wind without creating the turbulence that solid barriers can. For several decades we have known that farmsteads benefit from shelter belts. Now researchers at the United States Department of Agriculture Forest Service have measured the effect of general urban tree cover and have found that urban trees reduce wind in a neighborhood by nearly half.

Third, trees are renowned, particularly in arid regions, for being "evaporative coolers" which convert and dissipate incoming solar energy through evapo-transpiration processes. Although this property of trees is not fully understood, it holds the potential for being the most influential urban forest factor, possibly leading to the elimination of the urban heat island.

The Environment's Effect on Energy Use in Buildings

At the same time as we are realizing how trees affect the environment, we need to understand how environments influence energy use in buildings.

The main consequence of sunlight on building energy use is the solar gain which directly enters through windows, especially in northern regions where we insulate our roofs and walls. Fortunately, although it is complex, the path of the sun is quite predictable, so we clearly know the directions that are most important to control or permit solar gain throughout the year.

Visualize the three-dimensional path the sun takes, from its summer route of rising in the northeast, moving directly overhead, and setting in the northwest, to its shorter winter route low in the southern sky. At the same time realize that the more perpendicular the angle is between the sun and a window, the more energy the sun's rays bring. It should not be surprising that at this latitude the most intense solar energy strikes windows when the sun is low in the sky, having the most solar power on south windows at midday in September through March, and nearly as much intensity when the sun's rays strike east windows at 8 to 9 A.M. and west windows at 5 to 6 P.M. in April through August.

As the sun heats the surrounding air, this heat can be conducted directly through windows and walls. Because outdoor heat builds gradually throughout the day, a time lag exists with both outside and inside air overheating in the late afternoon. People indoors experience the most discomfort at this time of day and are most likely to turn on air-conditioning. The resulting high demand for summer air-conditioning in late afternoon overlaps with our society's tendency to come home from school and work and turn on our televisions and microwaves. Thus, peak demand for electricity occurs towards evening on the hottest days of the year. For most electrical utilities and the consumers who pay their bills, not only does this peak power directly cost more, but it is the primary reason for construction of new power plants which raises the cost of electricity. Consequently, a high priority for many in saving energy is to reduce peak loads.

The wind is another environmental factor which affects energy use in buildings. Unfortunately, the direction of the wind is less precise than that of the sun. Prevailing west and northwest winds in the winter and southerly breezes in the summer exist in most of the Upper Midwest, but these tendencies can be violated almost as much as they are followed. Nonetheless, the stronger the wind and the leakier the building, the more outside air will blow in and replace the inside air. This effect is most accentuated when the difference between indoor and outdoor temperatures is the greatest. When it is very cold outside in winter, the impact of wind is most severe. Conversely, in the summer, when indoor-outdoor temperature differences in this climate are not as extreme, wind is less of a factor. Needless to say, where natural ventilation is the means of summer cooling, care must be taken not to block these breezes.

Locating Trees for Energy Conservation

All of us intuitively know that trees make our environment more comfortable. Unfortunately, for most people the desire to do the right thing is not yet matched with the knowledge of how to do it right.

Shading Buildings A primary goal when planting landscape trees is to maximize shade during the summer and minimize shade during the winter. For homes and small commercial and institutional buildings, our objective is to maximize shade on windows during the cooling season at the times of day of greatest solar gain without decreasing solar gain during the heating season through windows when they receive the most intense sun.

The most effective location for shade trees is to the west and slightly north of west-facing windows, to provide late afternoon summer shade while minimizing winter shade on the windows. Trees placed to the east of east-facing windows are of the next greatest value for direct shade on buildings in summer.

Strictly from a building shading viewpoint (without recognizing the many other reasons for having trees), the least advantageous location for a tree is out in a yard south of a home where it provides no shade to the house in summer when the sun is overhead, and yet it shades the house in the winter when the sun is lower in the sky to the south. Computer studies done at the University of Minnesota which simulate tree shade on buildings suggest that for buildings with roof overhangs, trees placed south of the building are more likely to have negative winter effects than positive summer effects.

Trees should be selected which let the greatest amount of light through their branches in the winter and provide the greatest amount of shade in the summer. For the Upper Midwest, the most solar-friendly trees are deciduous species, setting leaves in early May, losing leaves in late September, and having sparse branches in winter. The further north an area, the more advantageous are trees which leaf out later and drop their leaves earlier. Good choices are Kentucky coffee tree, walnut, butternut, and ash. Moderately solar friendly trees include sugar and red maple. Among the less solar-friendly are oaks which retain their leaves in the winter and evergreens.

Shading Other Areas In addition to shading buildings directly, other uses of shade trees are likely to be beneficial. Providing tree shade to air-conditioning units (without blocking airflow around them) is likely to help them run more efficiently. Providing shade for parked cars is likely to reduce the amount they need to be cooled when started. In turn, these reductions in air conditioner use will also reduce the production of other air-polluting by-products.

Windbreaks Studies indicate that both trees planted in windbreaks and general tree cover can beneficially reduce wind. Unless they will shade a neighboring structure, on a residential lot place one or more rows of evergreen trees (8 to 10 feet on center in rows 15 to 20 feet apart) to the west and north of a building. On larger lots use more rows in the windbreak with the trees spaced 15 to 20 feet apart. Trees selected for windbreaks should be dense, relatively stiff, reasonably fast growing, and those that tend to keep their branches to the ground. Among the species often suggested are Norway spruce, white pine, and Colorado spruce.

The most critical factor for northern gardeners to recall when planting for energy conservation is that we live in a climate dominated by the need to heat buildings. While our summers are undoubtedly hot, we need to remember that Minnesota home owners typically spend 10 times more on heating than on cooling, even in a fully air-conditioned home. Some locations of trees can cost us more in heating fuel than they save in cooling reductions. Thus, to gain the most from trees, we should plant strategically to shade our homes and to shelter us from winter winds.

Mapping Your Home Landscape

Jane McKinnon

utting a landscape plan on paper is the most efficient way to design or remodel your home grounds. This article outlines a step-by-step process to help you make a scale drawing of your property. This drawing will help you select and properly locate the right kind of trees and shrubs for your yard.

If you prefer to hire a landscape architect, landscape designer, or commercial nursery firm to prepare plans for you, it is still important to organize your own ideas. A clear understanding between you and the designer is vital if you want a landscape plan that fits your property and the way you expect to use your outdoor space.

Equipment

You can draw your own plans using familiar tools and a few new items available from an office supply or stationery store. To prepare your base plan, the following items will be useful:

- A 50 to 100 foot measuring tape
- Note pad and pencil for recording measurements
- Graph paper (four squares to an inch is the most practical

- Tracing paper
- Masking tape for fastening tissue paper over the map
- A 12-inch ruler for measuring and for use as a straight edge in drawing
- Soft pencils and a gum eraser
- A plastic template with measured circles is convenient for drawing plants at their accurate size for proper spacing.

Mapping to Scale

The average residential lot is most easily mapped using a ¼ inch equals 1 foot scale. This scale allows for plenty of detail without creating an overly large plan. If you have a larger lot, you may need to use a ⅛ inch to 1 foot scale.

To get started creating your base map, you need to select a reference point from which to begin measuring. In many cases the corner of the house works best. Your goal is to locate everything as accurately as you can. You want your base map to include these features:

- Property lines, including any easements or rights-of-way.
- Your house, showing windows, doors, steps, walkways, decks,

patios, or porches.

- Garage, shed, or any other structures.
- Driveways, with connection to the street or the road.
- Utility poles, wires, underground pipes and utility connections.
- Fences, dog pens, etc.
- Natural landscape features such as rocks, water, or significant changes in elevation.
- A north point (preferably on top)
- Direction of prevailing winds and the path of the sun across the property.
- All existing trees and shrubs you plan on keeping.

As you're taking your measurements, start thinking about the different views you have of your property. As you walk up the driveway or front walk, is the view pleasing? What do you like about it? What don't you like about it? As you're walking the outside boundaries, stop and look out at the street and adjoining properties. What do you see from there? Walk up the street and look at your property from your neighbor's perspective.

What views do you have from inside the house? Look at the view from each room and make notes on what you like and don't like.

Pay attention to shadows. Make notes on which areas of your yard are sunny at different times of the day. Are some areas always in the shade? Make a note.

From the measurements recorded in your notebook, you can prepare your base map on the graph paper.

Trial Drawings

With an accurate base map and a detailed list of needs and considerations, you are ready to begin trial drawings. You will need a generous supply of tracing paper. Tape or tack a sheet of the paper over your map and experiment by drawing in rough circles around the areas of your yard that have or will have different uses. Three kinds of uses are often marked. First, space must be identified for the entrance or public area of your property - the land between your house and the street or the road. Next, mark off areas you need for work space. Third, mark off the living spaces that your family intends to use.

Sketching It In

Now it's time to start sketching in the sites for the trees and shrubs you plan on incorporating into your design. Using your circle template, draw circles to represent your chosen materials — when fully grown! This will make it much easier to estimate both the quantity of plants needed for a given space and will help keep you from crowding.

THE NORTHERN GARDENER'S LIBRARY

Chapter 2

Landscaping With Trees

Trees to Consider

Landscape Diversity

Trees for Creative Landscaping

Shade Trees:
Planting for the Future

Northern Natives

Trees to Consider

Fred Glasoe

I always enjoy noting the trees and shrubs which line the roads and surround the buildings I pass when I am out for a drive. However, because I see the same varieties and combinations over and over, I can't help but wonder what can be done to stimulate imagination and interest in good landscaping, and what can be said to encourage folks to make full use of the plants available.

The most evident landscaping problem right now is the use of too many of the same kinds of low cost, fast growing plants. Too often we pass by prime candidates for landscape plants because of price or a lack of knowledge about what is available. If folks would take the time to educate themselves and then make reasonable requests from nurseries and landscapers, a wider range of plants would become available.

Today we hear many calls for a return to the original plant life the pioneers knew. Yet, at the same time, plant breeders are working hard to develop new varieties of trees and shrubs that will be reliably hardy in USDA Zones 3 and 4.

I prefer a mixture of both the native and the new in my landscape. I shudder to think how many beautiful landscapes would be missing from our view if we had only planted native species. We would be almost without evergreens in over two-thirds of the state. Our summer scene would be without the bright colors of hardy azaleas and rhododendrons, hybrid lilacs, shrub roses, crab apples, and hundreds of significant others. We'd miss the juicy, sweet bites of apples, pears, and plums which we can now grow in our own back yards. Today we can expand our choices with hardy trees from many areas of the world. Breeders have developed new shapes, colors, and sizes by combining what we have with what they have found elsewhere in the world.

Let's look at a few new ideas for spring planting. Everyone who has a new home, as well as everyone who has a forty-year-old home which has become overgrown with original plantings, is a prospective customer. If I were going to plant a large shade tree this year, I would be most interested in white oak (*Quercus alba*) or swamp white oak (*Q. bicolor*). People have been so frightened by oak wilt that many of us will not even look at oaks. Providing you are not living in an area already heavily populated with oaks, these native species will be perfect shade trees and will remain for many generations.

Another shade tree we have been taught to avoid is the elm. Good news has arrived from breeders. Varieties have been developed which are resistent to Dutch elm disease. I am told there will be a new cultivar available this year called 'Cathedral' which grows about 40 feet. It should make a good replacement for our dying American elms.

The object of most Minnesotans' desires is the maple. Red maple (*Acer rubrum*) has bright orange and red fall color which makes it a dream tree for almost every yard. A new hybrid, 'Autumn Blaze' maple, is a cross between red maple and silver maple. It combines the best of both worlds by exhibiting good red fall color and fast growth. This is just the first of many new *Acer x freemanii* crosses which I am told will be moving into the nursery market in the next few years.

It has long been my feeling that there are far too many seedless ash trees in the Upper Midwest, and many are being infected with ash yellows, leaf drop, or one of the other problems associated with these trees. People are too conscious of seed production, viewing it as a detriment. There are many excellent hardy, disease-free trees which are unnecessarily avoided because of a few falling seeds or nuts. Lovely trees such as linden, Kentucky coffee tree, Ohio buckeye, and butternut are tremendous attributes in any yard. Disease is unheard of on ginkgo trees. They are often perfect for large urban yards. They grow slowly and do not overspread. Ginkgos also make fine boulevard plantings.

New fast-growing red maple varieties will soon be available. (MSHS)

There are several other interesting trees which should be considered if you can provide them with the special growing conditions they need. Even though many of these will be difficult to locate, I'd like to mention a few. Blue beech (*Carpinus caroliniana*) is a beautiful tree which we rarely see in Minnesota yards. The same could be said of Korean mountain ash (*Sorbus alnifolia*). Autumn blaze pear (*Purus calleryana* 'Autumn Blaze') has outstanding crimson red fall color. This tree and the intriguing Russian hawthorne (*Crataegus ambigua*) would make perfect small trees for the person who likes to grow the unusual. Most Minnesotans have yet to see a cork tree (*Phellodendron amurense*). I will be seeking out a Turkish filbert (*Corylus colurna*) this spring, since I am told it is very adaptable to hot summers and cold winters and has no pest or disease problems.

Whenever Minnesotans discuss disease problems on trees, they are sure to address what has gone wrong with their crab apple leaves. In the past two or three years, many trees have ended up naked by August, while others continue to look fine until frost. Many of us are on the lookout for crab apples which keep good leaves throughout summer and hold their fruit well into winter. Right now my list includes 'Prairifire', which has dark red flowers and fruit; 'Sugar Tyme', with pink to white flowers and red fruit; and 'Harvest Gold', with white flowers and gold fruit.

As I have often stated, we do not plant enough evergreens. In a state that is leafless for a good six months of the year, these green wonders remind us that there is promise of future plant life. Evergreens provide us with Currier and Ives landscapes in our modern world, even without covered bridges. I have always enjoyed the big-needled pines and firs. White, Scotch, Austrian, Swiss mountain, and Norway red pines bring out the natural rugged facets of the northern winter. My favorite evergreen by far is the white or concolor fir. It is a needled beauty which is truly rare in form and color.

We need to plant trees to beautify the landscape, to produce oxygen and help purify the air, to evaporate and purify our limited supply of fresh water, and to provide lumber, paper, and healthy fruits to eat. This is to say nothing of trees to climb and sit under while we enjoy the wonders of creation.

Landscape Diversity

John Ball

ith all the talk of cultural diversity these days, think about applying some of the same theory to your landscape. Drive through almost any residential neighborhood in the Upper Midwest and look at the trees. What do you see? Yard after yard shadowed by a random planting of ash trees, perhaps a linden, maybe a honeylocust, or one of the many cultivars of Norway maple.

Our reliance on such a limited number of species is cause for concern, a lesson not completely learned from our recent experience with elms and Dutch Elm disease. When we plant too many of the same species in an area, we are providing a large and convenient food supply for an insect or disease. The resulting damage is not limited to a tree or two, but to entire regions of a community, state, or country. Concentrations of single species can lead to pest and disease problems. Why not diversify the landscape with an array of different trees and shrubs?

Even given the limitations of our northern climate, there are sugar maples, hackberries, and several other trees you are probably familiar with, but the purpose of this article is to introduce you to a few trees you might not know. I call them my five favorite little-known trees.

I have selected these trees based on my personal observations of their performance in southern Minnesota, their ornamental value, and their size. These trees survived the very cold winter of 1982-83; they have interesting, and sometimes unique, ornamental potential; and several are relatively small. As you read through my list you will notice that most of these trees have a mature height of 25 to 40 feet, just the right size for a typical house on a quarter-acre lot.

These trees may be difficult to locate at a nursery, but are not impossible to find. And while these trees have few pest problems today, they may develop them in the future. Their relative pest-free nature may be because of their rarity in the landscape rather than any inherent resistance. The idea is to use them along with the species that are currently popular, thereby reducing the concentrations of any single species.

Amur Maackia (*Maackia amurensis*).

If you want a small tree (20 to 30 feet) with white, mid-summer flowers, look no further. This native of Manchuria has performed quite well in our northern climate. In addition to its late season flowers, it has several other desirable characteristics. The bark is a shiny, copper brown and the new leaves have a grayish-green color when they unfold. The leaves are pinnately compound with seven to eleven leaflets. There is no fall color.

The flowers, however, are the major ornamental asset. The small pea-shaped flowers occur in clusters, four to six inches long, during the last two weeks in July. The flowers are followed by pods that remain on the tree for the remainder of the year.

European Alder (*Alnus glutinosa*).

This tree has several ornamental assets, especially the pine cone-like fruits that remain on for several years. They are particularly showy during the winter months when the foliage is absent. It is well-suited to wet soil conditions and is a good choice for marshy land. European alder may reach a height of 40 feet and has a rapid growth rate during its first ten years. The foliage is a dark, glossy green; the leaves are rounded and coarsely toothed.

Blue beech (*Carpinus caroliniana*).

Many people think only of flowering trees when they are shopping for ornamental interest. Floral displays are often brief, while there are trees like the blue beech that offer longer lasting ornamental beauty.

The tree's most distinctive quality is its bark—smooth, bluish-gray, and fluted. The bark is especially showy when the tree is grown as a clump. The tree also has small-toothed oval leaves that turn yellow, orange, or scarlet in the fall.

Blue beech generally reaches a height of 20 to 30 feet, although it does not reach that height very fast, perhaps growing six to ten inches per year. The tree will grow best if planted in moist, slightly acid soil that is partially shaded by taller trees, but I have also seen it perform well in open, sunny yards.

Ironwood (*Ostrya virginiana*).

While common in oak forests throughout southern Minnesota, this small tree is almost never seen in residential plantings. As with blue beech, ironwood does not have an ornamental flower, but instead owes its ornamental value chiefly to its curly bark.

The bark of ironwood is broken into long, narrow, vertical strips that often break free at both ends. These slight curls add dimension to the bark texture. The foliage of ironwood is very similar to that of blue beech—the leaves are about the same size and shape, but offer little or no fall color.

Ironwood is a small, slow-growing tree. The mature height is about 25 to 35 feet, with an average yearly growth rate of one foot. The form is somewhat pyramidal. It prefers the same growing conditions as the blue beech. Ironwood is considered to be a relatively pest-free tree, although concentrated plantings have been susceptible to pests. Compacted soil and too much sun could cause stress.

Ironwood is planted chiefly for its interesting bark texture. (MSHS)

Blue ash *(Fraxinus quadrangulata).* If you want to plant an ash, why not plant a blue ash instead of the more commonly planted green ash? The big difference between blue and green ash is the form and bark pattern. Green ash generally has an irregular crown form; the lower branches have a weeping, almost contorted outline. Blue ash has a rounded crown, generally a single leader, and spreading branches. The bark is scaly, as opposed to the diamond-shaped furrows found on green ash. The twigs are much stouter, four-sided, and have a corky wing to them.

Blue ash is native to the dry, limestone soils of the eastern United States. While not indigenous to the Upper Midwest, it appears winter hardy throughout southern Minnesota. It reaches a height of about 25 feet in 15 years, with a mature height of about 45 feet as compared to 60 feet for green ash.

The list does not have to stop here. There are many other useful, but rarely used, trees. Kentucky coffeetree *(Gymnocladus dioicus)*, Amur cork tree *(Phellondendron amurense)*, and swamp white oak *(Quercus bicolor)* are all good possibilities.

Trees for Creative Landscaping

Terry Schwartz

Even though the list of trees available for landscaping goes on and on, most homeowners seem to select the same ones over and over. The following list includes a few different selections for you to consider. All are Zone 4 plants and hardy throughout the northern area, with the exception of techny arborvitae which is hardy to Zone 3. Most are fairly new, but some of them have been around for a while. Any of them would make attractive additions to a northern landscape.

Toba Hawthorn How would you like a small tree with clusters of double white flowers that last for up to 15 days, have a sweet scent, and fade to a soft pink? In late fall, small, bright red, marble-sized "apples" appear and hang on throughout the winter into early spring. It is not a flowering crabapple. It is *Crataegus mordenensis* 'Toba'. If you are not familiar with the hawthorns, you are missing out on one of the most exciting group of trees for the home landscape. Today's hawthorns are thornless and make exceptional landscape trees. Their trilobed foliage is virtually disease free, and the olive green to bronze-colored bark resembles the blue beech or musclewood tree. The ultimate height is 15 to 20 feet, making it perfect for the small yard.

I have a toba next to my deck that puts on a show of color after the flowering crabs are done. The flowers last much longer, and they are not bothered by high temperatures or winds that fade many crabapple flowers.

Korean Mountain Ash Another plant used far too little in the home landscape is *Sorbus alnifolia*, or Korean mountain ash. It is much more resistant to fireblight and sunscald then either *S. aucuparia* or *S. decora*. Sometimes referred to as densehead mountain ash, this tree has interesting speckled bark and is covered with the same bright orange-red berries that we associate with the European mountain ash. It is much better suited as a shade tree than the other mountain ash varieties because of its larger size (30 to 40 feet). The blossoms, which are car-

Korean mountain ash produces showy white flowers in late May. (MSHS)

ried high on this pyramidal-shaped tree, are outstanding in early spring. The last, and certainly not least, outstanding feature is its bright orange-red fall color.

Shamrock Linden One of the newest lindens to come along in the last few years is *Tilia cordata* 'Baleyi' or shamrock linden. Shamrock is a stately tree that is excellent for street plantings, as well as home use. The conical shape is somewhat similar to greenspire linden, but it has slightly larger leaves and is not quite as dense, resulting in more filtered shade. The branches are stout and uniformly spaced around the trunk, giving it a very formal appearance. It will reach 40 to 50 feet in height.

Deborah Maple *(Acer platanoides).* One tree that makes an attractive shade tree because of its color, as well as its stature, is a new introduction called Deborah maple ('Deborah'). This is an outstanding new variety of Norway maple that was selected from the more commonly known Schwedler maple in Vancouver, British Columbia in 1972. One of Deborah's best characteristics is its new growth that starts out a beautiful ruby red, changes to a deep maroon, and eventually turns green.

Like most Norway maples, it has a tall oval crown. The mature foliage is thick and leathery, making Deborah more resistant to sunscorch than most varieties of Norway maple. The canopy of the tree is very dense because of the numerous branches that develop from the main trunk. Deborah is a tree that transplants easily and is a fast grower, making it an ideal tree for homeowners looking for a quality specimen that will remain in their yards for years to come.

Redmond Linden For a truly formal appearance, Redmond linden (*Tilia americana* 'Redmond') is without a doubt one of the finest shade trees available to northern

Techny Arborvitae is fast growing and very winter hardy. It makes an excellent screen and hedge. (Hohman)

gardeners. Redmond linden has large, clean foliage typical of American linden. Its ultimate height is from 40 to 60 feet. Redmond is a very straight growing tree that forms a very definite pyramidal shape early and retains it until maturity.

An interesting winter characteristic is the branches of the previous year's new growth which are all tipped in red. Another thing this tree has going for it is that it is carried by many garden centers and nurseries.

Techny Arborvitae The only evergreen in this group, techny arborvitae (*Thuja occidentalis* 'Techny') has deep blue-green foliage. It is very tolerant of shearing, lending itself to use in very formal gardens, but can also be left as a graceful, unsheared hedge. It can be trained into a globe shape, which is another way it is sold. The biggest advantage to techny arborvitae, though, is that it does not winter burn once established and comes through our winters looking like it was on vacation in Florida. It is used much more in commercial plantings than the pyramidal arborvitae and for good reason. It is much more adaptable and can tolerate a wider range of extreme conditions. While there are many selections of arborvitae on the market, techny is the best choice for cold climates.

Shade Trees: Planting for the Future

Terry Schwartz

ollar for dollar, trees are the best investment a homeowner can make. The shade of a well-placed tree can cut summer cooling costs up to 50 percent. In the winter, a hedge or windbreak can reduce heating costs significantly. As much thought should be given to the selection and placement of shade trees as is given to planning the rest of the home. Trees may outlive the house itself, and will almost surely be there longer than the carefully chosen carpet and wallpaper.

If you live in an older home surrounded by mature trees, you've already got a good start. But if you're building a new home or if it's time to clean out the dead wood (so to speak), don't miss the chance to make the most of selecting the right trees for your home landscape. If your budget doesn't cover the cost of putting in shade trees, maybe you had better reconsider your priorities.

Here is a list of what I consider to be the best shade trees for home use in the Upper Midwest. Look them over, visit your local nursery, and decide which are the best for you.

Red Maple *(Acer rubrum)*.

Sometimes called swamp maple, red maple is a native tree that grows in moist locations and prefers a somewhat acidic soil. Fairly fast growing, it has soft, gray bark and an oval-shaped head. It has showy red flowers in the spring and the leaves turn bright red or yellow in the fall.

'Firedance' and 'Northwood' are two good cultivars. A columnar form, 'Autumn Spire', introduced by the University of Minnesota, is very upright and turns bright red in the fall.

Sugar Maple *(Acer saccharum)*.

Sugar maple is probably most famous for its maple syrup. The largest of all of our native maples, it usually turns brilliant yellow in the fall. Some trees turn scarlet, depending on soil conditions and the individual tree. The only way to be guaranteed a certain fall color is to buy a cultivar specifically introduced for a predictable fall color.

While there are many cultivars of this tree available, I still feel that the species is as good as any. This is

Sugar maples are large trees with broad-spreading crowns. (Hohman)

especially true in northern areas where many of the southern-introduced cultivars are not hardy enough. 'Bonfire' is a hardy cultivar that is very tolerant of heat and has a broad, oval shape.

Norway Maple *(Acer platnoides)*.

Norway maple should only be planted in the southern one-half to two-thirds of Zone 3. There are dozens of cultivars from which to choose. The popular 'Crimson King' has bright red leaves all summer long. Perhaps the hardiest and best Norway maple is 'Emerald Lustre'. This tree has dark, emerald green leaves and a very rounded, oval head at matu-

rity. I have never met anyone that doesn't think this is an outstanding tree.

River Birch *(Betula nigra)*.

Another native of Minnesota, river birch is found growing in river bottomlands, but does well in upland situations. It has beautiful bronze bark along with fantastic yellow fall color. One of its most desirable characteristics is its resistance to the bronze birch borer. It does well as a landscape tree and is much longer-lived than the paper birch. Like the paper birch, this tree lends itself well to growing as a clump. 'Heritage' is a good cultivar with whiter bark than the species.

Green Ash *(Fraxinus pennsylvanica)*.

Green ash has been over-planted in certain areas but is nonetheless an excellent shade tree. It is extremely hardy and has nice fall color. Some people think that ash flower gall is too much of a problem, but many trees never get the disease.

There are dozens of good cultivars to choose from. Here are a few in order of my preference:

'Marshall's Seedless'. As its name states, this is a seedless cultivar. At maturity, 'Marshall's Seedless' has a beautiful oval head that casts a good amount of shade. The shiny green foliage makes this tree outstanding.

'Summit'. This is a tree that is somewhat columnar in shape and has a very straight trunk. It is hardy in all areas and is seedless.

'Bergeson'. This selection, developed by Melvin Bergeson of Fertile, Minnesota, is fast growing and grows denser with age. It has a very straight trunk and is a good choice for home or boulevard use. It is seedless and the leaves turn yellow in the fall.

'Prairie Spire'. This selection from North Dakota is an extremely hardy tree and very compact. It is columnar in shape when young and becomes pyramidal with age.

Oak *(Quercus* spp)*.* Whenever I mention oaks as landscape trees, there is still the misconception that they have long tap roots that make them impossible to transplant. With modern nursery practices, these trees are grown with a fibrous root system that would make an ash envious. Nursery oaks can be transplanted with the ease of any shade tree.

This is not true for trees that have been collected from the wild, however. Most of those trees will die, and those that do live are so poorly branched that they will never develop into a good shade tree. Besides that, digging from public lands is illegal and depletes a natural resource that belongs to everyone, not only us, but future generations as well.

Oaks are easy to transplant and grow faster than you think. (MSHS)

Don't overlook oaks for your landscape. They are long-lived trees that will give generations of pleasure. Few trees provide shade as nicely as the venerable oaks. They are not as slow growing as you might think. Here are my three recommendations for oak varieties, all available from reputable growers:

Swamp White or Bicolor Oak *(Quercus bicolor).* This is a good tree for both wet and upland soil conditions. Ultimate height is 50 to 60 feet.

Pin Oak *(Quercus palustris).* The most vigorous growing of all the oaks, this tree makes an excellent specimen in the yard or boulevard.

Ultimate height is 40 to 60 feet.

Burr Oak *(Quercus macro-carpa)*. A vigorous grower as oaks are concerned, the burr oak has a semi-rounded form and corky branches. It is very tolerant of different soil types and air pollutants. Ultimate height is 60 to 80 feet.

Korean Mountain Ash

(Sorbus alnifolia). Reaching 30 to 40 feet in height, Korean mountain ash is a shapely tree that has attractive flowers in May. Scarlet berries appear in September and October and are eaten readily by the birds. This tree is sometimes sold as densehead mountain ash.

America Basswood or Linden *(Tilia americana)*.

The American linden is perhaps the finest tree in this genus. More than an excellent shade tree, some of the finest honey comes from its flowers. An excellent tea can be made from the flowers also. Wide and oval in its mature shape, this is a tree under which family reunions can be held.

Littleleaf Basswood or Linden *(Tilia cordata)*.

There are many excellent cultivars of this European introduction available. Littleleaf linden does very well in poor soils. Bees love its fragrant spring flowers. A very dense-growing tree, it is pyramidal in shape. Perhaps two of the best-known cultivars are 'Shamrock' and 'Greenspire'. 'Greenspire' is the denser of the two.

Imperial Locust *(Gleditsia triacanthos inermis* 'Imperial'*)*.

More compact than other cultivars, I think 'Imperial' is the nicest locust for the yard. It has a broad, spreading shape that creates fine, lacy shade. It is also seedless and thornless. When I planted one in my yard, I had to use a pick to get through the limestone and compacted soil. I used no special soil and the tree is thriving. It has not shown any sign of stress, even with the drought conditions of the late 1980s. To say that it likes hot, dry conditions and is tolerant of poor soil is an understatement!

Remember, careful thought and planning of your home landscape will be a benefit to you and those who will follow in the years to come. Learning to think more carefully about the environment means thinking not just about the trees and plants, but thinking of the people who will follow us and the world we will leave them. With the destruction of valuable forests and plant life around the world, the urban landscape will play an increasingly important role in cleaning the air that we breathe.

Northern Natives

Terry Schwartz

hen looking for new cultivars for our area, one of the first places growers are now looking is in their own backyard, so to speak. Some of the best plant material is found in native stands, and because it is native, it is usually very hardy and disease-resistant. When it comes to looking for hardiness, good fall color, and other desirable landscape traits, it is best to start with what is already thriving in this area.

For example, a selection of red maple chosen for beautiful fall color from a southern state will perform poorly or may not even survive a harsh, northern winter. A selection of the same plant made from northern Minnesota will survive anywhere in the north as well as the south. It is likely to show its fall color up to two to three weeks earlier than a southern selection. The typically shorter growing season causes the northern selection to harden off and enter dormancy much earlier than those grown further south. If the two selections were growing side by side in a yard, in early October you would see the northern selection ablaze with color, while its southern counterpart would still think its summer and be either totally green or just beginning to show signs of color.

Much work is being done by universities and nursery growers in Canada and the northern United States to develop or find plants that are well-adapted to northern climates, resulting in a growing list of northern selections for your yard.

White Ash *(Fraxinus americana* 'Autumn Purple'*)*. With their outstanding fall color, I find it very refreshing to see the new cultivars of white ash and black ash becoming available. Although it is not really that new, 'Autumn Purple' has not become very well known. Locally grown trees can be identified by their deep purple fall color. The branching habit results in an attractive oval shape, and the smooth, gray bark makes an interesting statement in the landscape. Like most trees in this species, it can tolerate moist soil conditions. 'Autumn Purple' is a seedless selection, a desirable characteristic for most homeowners who want to

'Autumn Purple' is a rapid grower with a shapely oval crown. (MSHS)

Ultimate height of this tree is around 50 to 60 feet. Two desirable landscape features are its low pruning requirements and its light seed production.

Black Ash *(Fraxinus nigra 'Fallgold')*. One interesting aspect of using native plant material is the history that accompanies it. Many of our native plants were highly valuable to American Indians and early settlers. Black ash was cut, the bark removed, and the log pounded to loosen the annual rings, which were separated and used to make baskets.

'Fallgold', another Canadian introduction, has very dark green foliage, strong crotches, and is a vigorous grower. Like other black ash, it turns a vivid golden yellow in early fall. The tree is very easy to care for, with its low pruning requirements. Another real asset is the fact that it is also seedless. If you compare the foliage to that of the commonly grown green ash, you will find the black ash has a more concave leaf, making it much more interesting in appearance. The tree will reach heights of 50 to 60 feet, and spread 15 to 20 feet. The leaves hang on longer in fall than most other trees of this species.

avoid messy seeds. The only drawback to this cultivar is that it is not hardy in Zone 3 and therefore not recommended north of the Twin Cities area.

White Ash *(Fraxinus americana 'Autumn Blaze')*. This selection of white ash is considered hardy to Zone 3, so listen up all you northern, northern gardeners. Like 'Autumn Purple', this more recent Canadian introduction has a typical oval form and turns a beautiful purple color in the fall. It comes to us from the Morden Research Station in Manitoba, and was introduced by the Canadian Ornamental Plant Foundation.

Gray Dogwood (Tree form) *(Cornus racemosa)*. Found throughout Minnesota, gray dogwood is most commonly thought of as a shrub. However, when grown in a tree form, it takes on a distinction all its own. Its straight trunk and well-developed branches make for a very attractive small tree. It also provides quite an impressive display of creamy white flowers in the spring. The white fruit produced in September are very attractive to birds. Both the flowering and fruiting are enhanced when this plant is grown as a tree, because of the reduced competition between the numerous branches of a shrub. Growing only to eight to ten feet, this is a welcome addition to our list of available small trees.

Red Maple *(Acer rubrum)*. Also known as swamp maple, this is an excellent choice for a shade tree, growing up to 60 feet tall. It prefers a slightly acidic, sandy loam soil and will not grow well on alkaline soils. It has beautiful red flowers borne in dense clusters in April, and its brilliant fall color ranges from yellow to red.

'Northwoods' and 'Firedance' are two new cultivars that color more consistently than the species. 'Northwoods', a University of Minnesota introduction, turns an orange-red color in the fall. 'Firedance', the more recent introduction, turns a vivid scarlet every fall. Both are selections from northern Minnesota and are valuable additions.

Showy Mountain Ash *(Sorbus decora)*. Although this species is not as common as its European counterpart, *Sorbus aucuparia*, it is no less valued as a landscape plant. It is slightly smaller, reaching heights of only 15 to 20 feet, but the fruits are a brighter red and somewhat larger. This fully hardy tree also has larger leaves and tends to be somewhat cleaner than European mountain ash.

Canada Plum *(Prunus nigra)*. The only cultivar of Canada plum worth noting is 'Princess Kay', a University of Minnesota introduction, selected from Itasca County in northern Minnesota. This beautiful, double-flowered selection blooms in early May with ruby-red flower buds that open to white with a pink blush. Reaching heights of 15-20 feet, with bright red fruit in August, this tree is an excellent choice for small, but important, spaces. Canada plum is an excellent source of food for wildlife. In addition, the twigs and bark on young trees have prominent markings that, in combination with the black bark, add much winter interest.

THE NORTHERN GARDENER'S LIBRARY

Chapter 3

Landscaping With Shrubs

Shrubs to Consider

Shrubs for Shade

Northern Natives

Hardy Shrub Roses

Shrubs To Consider

Fred Glasoe

pring shrub selection and planting is the subject of this chapter. As with trees, early planting of shrubs helps them flourish because they begin growth in cool, moist weather and have the longest possible first-year growth period.

Buyers are often interested in almost anything that has a bargain price tag, grows fast, and needs minimal care. Yet, there are many other shrubs worth investigating.

Evergreens generally cost more than deciduous shrubs, but they are an asset to the landscape every month of the year. There are also many shrubs which provide a three season show. By careful selection, it is possible to create a small arboretum right in your own yard which will attract and entertain many fascinating birds and other two-legged creatures.

Rhododendrons open the

Azaleas are available in a wide range of colors. The 'Northern Lights' series is reliably hardy to -40 F. (Prilen)

spring bloom show, followed closely by Minnesota's own Northern Lights series of hardy azaleas. Use these shrubs, together with Korean and Chinese lilacs, in foundation plantings and as backgrounds in border gardens.

Also suitable for the mixed border are shrub roses. Many new hardy shrub roses are moving into the market. Among the newest and the best are 'Morden's Blush', 'Morden's Ruby', and 'McKinsey', all part of the Explorer series. Other favorites in this series are 'Martin Frobisher', 'Champlain', 'Cuthbert Grant', and the super hardy climber 'William Baffin'.

Some folks are looking for shrubs that will grow well in dry, sandy areas or in USDA Zone 3 landscapes. Two hardy shrubs which are not used as much as they should be are the common witch hazel *(Hamamelis virginiana)* and gray dogwood *(Cornus racemosa)*. Sometimes we look away from home for plants to fill the bill when they are right in our own "back yard."

Many people do not realize that we have a native deciduous holly in our state. Winterberry *(Ilex verticilata)* is a moisture-loving shrub with rich green leaves, white flowers, and red and orange berries which appear in August and September. Its berries attract birds, but be sure to plant both a male and a female shrub so you will get fruits from this dioecious shrub.

At the end of one of my perennial border beds I have a European compact viburnum *(Viburnum opulus* 'Nanum'). It is a mass of white balls of bloom in June, followed by red fruits that appear in August and remain through most of the winter. It is a real attention-getter, especially in a semi-shady area. All viburnums are excellent shrubs, both as specimens and as hedges, producing thick foliage which turns a vibrant color in fall. Tall types make excellent screens, without the root encroachment of the common lilac.

Hidden among the many rows of potted shrubs at the nursery are

Viburnums add color to the fall landscape. (MSHS)

some fine, but seldom used, plants. Look for the bright red-berried stems of coralberry *(Symphoricarpos orbiculatus)* or the always showy chokeberrry *(Aronia* species*)*, with its nice white early bloom followed by interesting bunches of black berries in fall and winter. This shrub also offers glossy green summer foliage which turns bright red in fall.

If you are blessed with a little extra room in your shade garden, don't pass up a very special favorite of mine – the pagoda dogwood *(Cornus alternifolia)*. It makes a truly unique specimen tree or shrub having a pagoda-like shape and offering both spring bloom and fall color.

Deep red flowers on 'Red Prince' weigela make it a garden must. It was developed at Iowa State University, and both its hardiness and its color are outstanding.

Spirea hybrids increase in popularity every year. The golden leaves of 'Goldmound' and 'Goldflame' are much sought after. 'Gold-mound' maintains its yellow leaves all season and fares better in mid-summer than the rust-stained foliage of the often oversold golden mock orange. Two small, but heavily flowered spireas, are 'Little Princess' and 'Alpine'. Both will provide long periods of mid-summer color in low borders and rock gardens.

As I page through nursery catalogs or travel south, I often see different trees and shrubs which would look great in my Minnesota yard. Invariably, when I look them up, they are listed as suitable for Zones 6, 7, or 8, and all of my desire flies out the window. There is no denying we are limited in this climate. Yet, Zones 3 and 4 are suitable for some very fine plants which most home owners know little about and never see. The plants are out there! Some may cost a little more, but it is worth shopping for good, locally grown species which will improve your living environment and increase your property value.

Gardening Skill

The ability to grow any acid-loving plant depends greatly on the site selection and preparation.

Because of their shallow, fibrous root systems, azaleas and rhododendrons require a soil that is uniformly moist, but not saturated. Organic soils and light, well-drained soils should be avoided. Heavy, poorly drained soils will result in loss of plants to root rot.

In addition to the physical soil requirement azaleas and rhododendrons require an acid soil with the pH in the range of 4.5 to 5.5 for best results.

Shrubs for Shade

Kate Hintz

Is your house surrounded by a beautiful canopy of tall trees? The trade-off might be grass that no longer grows under the maples, scraggling junipers that thrived under the hot sun of years past, and sun-loving flowering shrubs planted beneath the trees that refuse to bloom or even grow.

Or is yours a new home, waiting for shrubs to be planted on either side of the front door? The nursery offers a magnificent collection of fragrant lilacs and colorful purple-leaf sand cherries. On impulse, you buy several sand cherries, take them home, and plant them on either side of the front door on the north side of your house. The plants grow a little, but are never as beautiful as the weekend they were purchased.

Avoid either of these scenarios by assessing the microclimate of your yard and choosing plants whose cultural requirements match your site. First, consider the amount of sun and shade your yard receives. Then match individual locations to plants with similar cultural requirements. Be especially careful in shady locations where those tempting flowering shrubs struggle to grow and refuse to bloom.

Shady areas are characterized by the degree of light they receive, ranging from full shade, filtered shade, to half or light shade. By pruning the lower branches of a tree, you may be able to decrease the amount of shade in an area, but for the most part, you will have to plant according to available light.

Dense shade is found under a mature maple where the ground receives no direct sunlight. An area with light shade, often found on the east side of a home, receives good light and a few hours of sun. Filtered shade, such as that found under a stately elm, receives good light for most of the day.

Each shady area is unique. When considering a new planting of shrubs in a shady spot, first observe the location over a period of time, both throughout the day and throughout the growing season, if possible. Note the total amount of light received, when it comes, and how long it stays. Does the site receive at least a half day of full sun, or two hours of morning sun? Does the location get filtered light in the heat of the day? In addition, consider nearby plants—their color, form, and foliage. Lastly, envision the mature size of shrubs you are considering. That small shrub you plant under your window today may someday completely block the view from that window.

Which shrub will work in a certain location depends not only on available light, but also on available moisture. Big trees are thirsty plants, and many have roots which grow close to the soil surface, sapping up available surface water and nutrients. If you are going to plant shrubs under a canopy of trees, take the time to improve the soil. Add generous amounts of compost, manure, peat, sand, or whatever organic matter is available. After planting, apply a mulch annually to further conserve moisture and provide additional nutrients.

Once you have analyzed your location, begin considering the spectrum of shrubs that will tolerate less than full sun. The list includes shrubs with diverse form, foliage, fall color, flowers, and fragrance—all elements that add beauty and interest to your landscape throughout the seasons.

There are only a few shrubs that will flourish in dense shade. Your best bets are gray dogwood (*Cornus racemosa*), maple-leaved viburnum *(Viburnum acerifolium)*, nannyberry *(Viburnum lentago)*, and yew *(Taxus* spp.). Yew are one of the few evergreens that tolerate heavy shade, and the variety of upright, spreading, and dwarf forms available make them invaluable for shady landscapes.

The list of shrubs for light or filtered shade includes many more plants. For flowering shrubs, consider rhododendrons and azaleas—their pastel blossoms are set off beautifully when planted against a dark background. White-flowering varieties of viburnums and hydrangeas offer contrast as well. Weigela flowers sparkle pink or

Rhododendron 'PJM' provides early-season color. (MSHS)

red, blooming off and on throughout the summer. Variegated dogwood *(Cornus alba* 'Argenteomarginata'), although not a flowering shrub, has leaves that will flicker in the shade all summer long.

For color in the cool days of autumn, winged euonymus *(Euonymus alata)* and fragrant sumac *(Rhus aromatica)* turn brilliant red. Amur maple *(Acer ginnala)* is a compact shrub, whose glossy leaves turn to shades of yellow-orange and red in the fall, and its reddish fruits persist into winter. The flowers of witchhazel *(Hamamelis virginiana)* are a showy yellow in late October. Rhododendrons, which keep their leaves all winter, turn deep reddish-purple to provide winter color. In the autumn, nannyberry viburnum *(Viburnum lentago)* turns purplish-red and its blue-black berries serve as winter bird food.

Shrubs with fruits and fragrance add interest to the lightly shaded garden. The spicy, pale pink or white blossoms of *Clethra alnifolia* are guaranteed to attract attention in August. Cranberry cotoneaster *(Cotoneaster apiculatus)* and winterberry *(Ilex verticillata)* both have red berries that persist until January— or until hungry birds find them.

If you have the space, as well as cool, moist, acidic soil conditions in your shade garden, a pagoda dogwood *(Cornus alternifolia)* adds grace and elegance, with its hori-

Winged euonymus comes alive with fall color. (MSHS)

zontal spreading form. Lastly, the stems of red-osier dogwood *(Cornus sericea)* will contrast boldly with the snow in winter.

Shrubs are long lived and relatively difficult to move. Making the proper match of location and cultural requirements will save you disappointment. The wide range of shrubs that like shady sites makes the job a pleasure. Choose plants that satisfy your situation and your taste—you'll have it made in the shade.

Northern Natives

Terry Schwartz

In these days of Japanese barberry and Russian peashrubs, it's nice to know that there is a growing list of native shrubs available from local nurseries. Even though most of these plants are widely available, many go unnoticed because of a lack of awareness. Armed with a little more knowledge, homeowners can start to take advantage of these homegrown beauties.

Don't ignore the exotics—every new introduction for northern climates is a welcome one. But native plants have a special place in our landscapes—they offer a sense of home and history. Their easy care and natural look will also provide the homeowner with great satisfaction.

Serviceberry shrubs give a more natural look to the home landscape. (MSHS)

Juneberry or Serviceberry *(Amelanchier* spp.). Grown either as a large shrub or small tree, this native provides a striking display of white in early spring when nothing else is blooming. Growing 20 to 25 feet in height, the juneberry produces a small, berry-like fruit, which is a favorite of birds as well as jelly-makers. One cultivar worth mentioning is 'Regent'. This 4 to 6-foot shrub produces an abundance of fruit and has fall color, which changes from yellow to red.

Flame Willow *(Salix).*
Although not widely available, this plant is still worth mentioning. It displays exceptional orange-red twig color during the winter months. It is best suited for use as a

background or windbreak plant, rather than as a specimen plant. This variety of willow was discovered by Melvin Bergeson of Fertile, Minnesota.

Winterberry *(Ilex verticillata)*.
One of my personal favorites, and definitely under used, is winterberry or northern holly. The most noticeable and attractive feature is its scarlet fruit, produced in early October. Because this plant is dioecious (male and female flowers are on separate plants), you'll need several plants of both sexes to assure flower and fruit production. This deciduous shrub prefers a slightly acidic, sandy loam soil. It will reach heights of up to 10 feet, but can easily be kept pruned to 4 to 6 feet. Three currently available cultivars are 'Red Sprite', 'Winter Red', and 'After Glow'. All are generally more compact in growth habit than the species.

American Highbush Cranberry *(Viburnum trilobum)*.
This popular landscape plant has fruit that is very attractive to birds and is also suitable for jelly. At average heights of 10 to 12 feet, this large shrub is fully hardy and has trilobed leaves that turn a vivid scarlet in the fall. 'Alfredo' and 'Bailey Compact' are two popular cultivars. Both are more compact than the species and grow very dense without any special pruning. 'Alfredo' tends to bear more fruit. Both are excellent either as hedge or specimen plants.

Elders *(Sambucus* spp.).
While definitely too large for foundation plantings, elders are an excellent choice for attracting birds, creating a screen, or growing just for their attractive foliage. The elder is not generally known for the beauty of its foliage, but many people are not aware of the improved varieties of elder that are available.

Elders will tolerate moist soils, which makes them quite useful for planting along lakes, ponds, and streams. They will sucker, but this can be an advantage in naturalized plantings. Stem borers can sometimes be a problem, but because these plants are so vigorous, they usually outgrow any damage from the borer and come back even fuller than they were before.

Golden Locks Elder *(Sambucus racemosa* 'Golden Locks')**.** This is a cutleaf form of elder with deeply cut, golden-yellow leaves. It is a Canadian introduction from Morden Research Station. The foliage does not scorch as much as a similar cultivar, 'Sutherland Golden', making it a better plant for use in the home landscape.

Red Berried Elder *(Sambucus pubens)*. This shrub, growing to up to ten feet, bears yellowish-white flowers in spring and brilliant red berries in June. Although the berries are inedible for humans, the birds will gladly gobble them up.

Redman Elder *(Sambucus racemosa* 'Redman'*)*. This hardy Zone 4 plant, common in Canada, is finally finding its way to the northern United States. It can grow to be quite tall, reaching heights up to 20 feet. Its smooth, light brown branches hold a lot of bright red fruit in early May. Its most unique feature, however, is its deeply cut green foliage that is spectacular when adorned with the crimson fruit.

Adams Elder *(Sambucus canadensis* 'Adams'*)*. The fruit of the American elder is excellent for wines, pies, and jelly, and many people choose to grow it for these reasons alone. 'Adams', a cultivar from Union Springs, New York, was selected for its large clusters of blue to black fruit. This shrub flowers in late June and is excellent for use in wildlife plantings or for background use.

Golden Elder *(Sambucus canadensis* 'Aurea'*)*. This cultivar has foliage that rivals golden mockorange or any other yellow-leaved plant commonly seen in our landscapes. With its broad, golden-yellow leaves and red fruits, this plant is quite striking. It is a hardy, fast-growing shrub that should be considered, especially when you are looking for background material. Like any yellow-leaved plant, it needs full sun to produce its best color.

Dwarf Bush-Honeysuckle *(Diervilla Ionicera)*.

All but unheard of until just a few years ago, this shrub has gained in popularity in recent years. It is a small plant, reaching only four feet in height. Being both mound-shaped and spreading, it is an excellent plant for use in mass plantings or on slopes. I have one in a foundation planting and it performs quite well, even though it is generally not recommended for this use. Suckering can be a problem in a confined area, but can be controlled with a little maintenance pruning.

The foliage of dwarf bush-honeysuckle is a bronze-green color with small, delicate yellow flowers produced in early summer. It is very hardy and thrives on poor, dry soil. Removing the top two-thirds of the plant in early spring will produce a thick, rich carpet of neat foliage throughout the summer.

Hardy Shrub Roses

Terry Schwartz

oses have been the most sought after and adorned of all garden plants for centuries. In the last 100 years, however, most of the breeding work has centered around hybrid teas and other garden roses. Unfortunately, these are not hardy in our climate, creating a lot of extra work for the Northern gardener.

In recent times, more and more work has been devoted to the development of roses hardy in our climate. Much of this research is being done by our Canadian neighbors.

Exciting? You bet it is. Never before have so many new varieties of hardy shrub roses been available at the retail level. And, in the next few years, more will be introduced that will not only be useful in the home landscape, but in commercial plantings as well. Shrub roses that can appropriately be called ramblers will be appearing along freeways and on berms where in the past nothing else would grow.

In the following paragraphs, I have assembled a collection of hardy roses that are truly the gems of the rose world. What excites me most about these plants is their hardiness, low maintenance requirements, exquisite flowers, and spectacular foliage.

You will see in the descriptions of these varieties that many do grow quite large. For the Midwesterner used to the typical winter-dwarfed hybrid teas, this may take some getting used to. However, anyone who has lived in

Beautiful in bloom, hardy roses are a natural for the North. (Philstrom)

or visited other parts of the country knows that roses which grow 5 to 10 feet in height are not uncommon.

The "climbing" roses mentioned do not have tendrils and therefore need to be tied and trained on a trellis, fence, or some similar structure just like any other climbing rose.

Explorer Series

The Explorer series of roses was developed in Ottawa, Ontario, Canada, at the government research station. All of the varieties are named after Canadian explorers. The aim in the development of these roses was to combine winter hardiness with improved flowering and ornamental features. They have been tested in various parts of Canada, including the prairie provinces.

Alexander Mackenzie This 1984 introduction is a vigorous, upright shrub which can be used as a climber. It will grow to more than 6 feet in height. The foliage is shiny green and free of blackspot and mildew. This plant continues to produce cupped flowers on upright blooms throughout the season. Flower color is light red fading to deep pink. Fragrance is rated high on this extremely hardy plant.

David Thompson This compact shrub is a 1979 introduction of a rugosa hybrid. The large flowers, which appear throughout the summer right up until a frost, are double, purple-red, and have a pleasing scent. The mature height of this extremely hardy shrub is 4 to 5 feet. It is resistant to both blackspot and powdery mildew.

Henry Hudson This rose has a spicy-scented bloom that starts out as a pink bud and opens to a pure white flower with yellow stamens. It is highly resistant to powdery mildew as well as blackspot. This is a beautiful, low-growing rugosa hybrid that is 4 to 5 feet in height at maturity. Flowers appear repeatedly throughout the summer.

Jens Munk This cross between *R. rugosa "Schneezwerg" x R. rugosa* 'Frau Dagmar Hastrup' is very hardy as well as being resistant to blackspot and mildew. The fragrant, light pink, double flowers have yellow stamens. They appear on a vigorous plant that blooms heavily in June, July, and August. Ultimate height is around 5 feet.

Martin Frobisher This plant works very well as a flowering hedge. It is a vigorous, upright grower that reaches 6 feet in height. The yellow-green foliage is resistant to mildew and blackspot. It has soft pink blooms that appear throughout the season and are lightly scented. This plant is very hardy.

John Franklin This 1980 introduction is the least hardy of the explorer series, freezing back to about fifty percent in most winters. Lynn Colicutt of Morden Research Station in Manitoba, Canada, informed me that it is as hardy or hardier than several of the Parkland series roses, however, so it should do fine throughout most of Minnesota. Flowers are borne in clusters on a compact, low-growing shrub. The attractive, ruffled flowers appear throughout the season. They start out dark red and fade to pink before falling. It is resistant to mildew but not blackspot.

Henry Kelsey This attractive, red-flowering rose works well as a sprawling ground cover, but performs best as a climber. For Northern gardeners who love climbing roses but do not like to fight with them in the fall to cover them, this introduction is a godsend, as it needs no winter protection. Extremely vigorous, it blooms profusely until frost freezes the buds.

John Cabot The strong, arching branches of this pillar type of rose make it suitable as a large bush or a climber. Flowers open light pink and change to orchid as they mature. A pleasing fragrance and blooms which appear throughout the season make this a highly recommended, award-winning rose.

Meidiland Series

This group of shrub roses appeared on the market in the last two years in quantities large enough to make them readily available to everyone. They are called Meidiland (May D Land) shrub roses because they come from the House of Meidiland in France which has long been known for producing some of the finest roses in the world.

The Meidiland series has been tested in Europe as far north as Helsinki, Finland. While not thoroughly tested in North America, the plants I am familiar with in east central Minnesota have done fine for the past 2 years.

These roses are called shrubs because they are very vigorous, large plants with 4 to 6 foot spreads and long, arching branches. They are most often pictured as hedges or ground covers in garden catalogs, and for the most part, that is where they belong, rather than in foundation plantings.

Scarlet Meidiland This plant has velvety, scarlet flowers that bloom profusely for about a month in early summer and then continue with lighter blooming until frost. The flowers are double, up to 1 1/2 inches across, and appear in clusters at the end of the stems. The ultimate height of this shrub is about 4 feet with a spread of 6 feet.

Pink Meidiland This plant has a very pleasing clear pink flower with a white center. The single flowers are produced on an upright, bushy plant that will grow to be about 3 1/2 feet wide. It will bloom continuously up to frost and has attractive seed hips which remain throughout the winter.

Ferdy This is a stunning coral pink rose that blooms for a month in the spring with azalealike flowers. Its interesting foliage is almost fernlike. This plant also boasts an attractive red-orange fall color before it rests in the winter. Ultimate height is 3 1/2 to 5 feet; its width is around 3 to 4 feet.

White Meidiland Snow white, 4-inch double blossoms set off by dark green leathery foliage are just one reason to grow this beautiful shrub. White Meidiland has a low, mounding growth habit and will spread to 5 feet.

Bonica This is the only plant of this group I would recommend for use as a foundation plant as it is the smallest. It has many fine qualities that make it a winner. Three-inch blooms are borne in clusters which first appear in June. It appears that in Minnesota's climate this plant will perform similar to some of the Parkland Series roses, freezing to the snowline. Because of this, this plant will usually end up smaller than the 4 to 5 feet most catalogs list it as.

Bonica has been around longer than the other Meidiland roses, and consequently I have had more experience with it. The thing that stands out most in my mind is that

Many shrub roses continue to bloom well into the fall. (Hohman)

it is every bit as free a bloomer as 'Nearly Wild', another popular shrub rose. Bonica will be loaded with blooms right up until the time there is "frost on the pumpkin." This plant is worthy of its All-America rose selection honors.

The interest in hardy roses has grown rapidly over the past few years and for good reason. If you are interested in learning more about this exciting group of plant materials, may I suggest you read *Classic Roses* by Peter Beales.

On the following page is information on common diseases and basic growing tips.

Insects and Diseases of Shrub Roses

Aphids These small, green or blackish pests can overrun a rose garden in no time. Being sucking insects, they generally infest growing tips and will stunt and affect flowering. If the infestation becomes bad, recruiting an insecticide may be necessary to control the problem. Always follow manufacturers instructions.

Powdery Mildew This fungal disease shows up as a white powdery film on the foliage. If the infection becomes bad enough, the leaves will curl up and eventually fall off. Good air circulation around plants is the best way to prevent an outbreak of powdery mildew. A spray of a sulphur powder after hot, humid weather will also help prevent it.

Blackspot This fungal disease shows up as small black spots on the foliage and stems. Some varieties are more susceptible than others. A sulfur spray before symptoms appear will be of some help.

Spider Mites These little pests are not usually a problem unless hot and dry weather conditions exist for extended periods of time. Vigorous plants seldom have problems. The tiny mites are found on the undersides of the foliage and are visible by tapping the foliage onto a white piece of paper. A sign of their presence is a yellow discoloration of the foliage. A good, heavy spraying with the garden hose is generally enough to wash them off.

Culture of Shrub Roses

Hardy shrub roses require very little maintenance, no winter protection, and only minimal pruning. The most important factors in keeping roses healthy are good soil fertility, adequate moisture, plenty of sun, and good air circulation. If these few requirements are kept in mind at planting, your job of maintaining healthy plants will be much easier.

Roses will do best if they are grown in a well-drained, fertile soil. However, if the soil is allowed to become too dry, you will sacrifice flower numbers and size. A soil pH of 6.0 to 6.5 is optimum.

While mulching is not necessary for hardy roses, a plant grown under a mulch will be much less subject to stress than a plant grown under cultivated conditions. Like most plants, they will perform much better with a thick layer of wood chips, composted grass clippings, or whatever is available in your area for this purpose. Mulching protects the roots in a cold winter when there is minimal snow cover, and in the hot days of summer it preserves valuable moisture.

Chapter 4

Landscaping for Special Interest

Flowering Trees and Shrubs

Foundation Plantings

For the Birds

Landscaping for Wildlife

Fall Color

Winter Interest

Flowering Trees and Shrubs

Paul B. Kannowski

Fred Glasoe

Keeping a record of when your trees and shrubs flower in the spring is a little like creating your own almanac. Warm temperatures in early spring stimulate growth, but snow and cloudy weather can retard it. While nursery catalogs make spring flowering dates seem like scheduled events, in fact, there is much year-to-year variation.

The variation can be caused by winter snow cover, uneven snow melting, soil conditions in winter and spring, shade and wind protection, and damage to flower buds from freezing and thawing. Even plants of the same variety, growing in the same locality, may have different flowering times because of differences in sites and exposures.

For the past ten years, I've kept records of the time of first flowering for many of the plants in my yard in Grand Forks, North Dakota. The property is located in the flood plain of the Red River, a naturally wooded part of the city. The front yard faces west, is open with a large lawn and flower beds in front of the house and along the north and south boundaries. The back yard contains four mature American elm trees that provide considerable shade and an evergreen screen on the north boundary. Because prevailing winds tend to be northwesterly, the back yard is more protected than the front.

Grand Forks is located in the middle of Zone 3, which means that we can expect minimum winter temperatures in the -30° to -40°F range. The ground begins to freeze in early November and remains frozen until late March. Most of the trees, shrubs, vines, and perennial flowers in my garden are well-adapted to Zone 3. A few are of borderline hardiness, but those are located in sites that are protected from the wind.

I began keeping records of flowering dates in 1980 by recording species on a calendar. Initially, I had no plans for a long-term study. The records for the first four years were somewhat opportunistic, mainly of the most obvious plants. In 1984 I began to systematically collect data on all species and, for those species where I had several varieties, from selected varieties. Recently, I transferred all of my records to a database on my personal computer.

From a total of 127 species and varieties for which I have records, I have chosen 20 trees and shrubs for illustration of the flowering pattern.

Spring Flowering Dates of Trees and Shrubs

American elm
April 5 to 20

Forsythia 'Sunrise'
April 10 to 30

Nanking cherry
April 15 to May 5

PJM rhododendron
April 20 to May 10

Wild plum
April 22 to May 12

Wild gooseberry
April 20 to May 15

'Dolgo' crab apple
April 25 to May 30

Ohio buckeye
April 30 to May 20

Common lilac
April 30 to May 25

Tatarian honeysuckle
May 5 to May 15

Flowering quince
May 10 to May 15

Russian mulberry
May 1 to May 15

Redosier dogwood
May 5 to May 20

Blue holly
May 1 to May 20

Potentilla 'Abbotswood'
May 5 to May 30

Weigela 'Pink Princess'
May 5 to May 25

Lemoine Deutzia
May 5 to May 30

Preston lilac 'James Macfarlane'
May 5 to May 30

Amur maple
May 10 to May 30

Black raspberry
May 8 to May 30

Early spring is without a doubt the best time to plant new trees and shrubs. Small urban yards are often crowded with too many oversized shade trees which bury the home and overshadow the gardens. These can be replaced by any number of small trees which show off well without taking over the entire area with shade and serpentine root systems.

I have many favorite small trees which are both showy and easy to grow. Here are just a few:

• Many hawthorns (*Crataegus* spp.) as well as the blue beech (*Carpinus caroliania*) have interesting colors and showy forms that always appear well-kept.

• Ornamental fruit trees such as 'Meteor' cherry (a great pie-cherry producer), the orange-berried mountain ash, and the many spring-flowering crab apples stand out well as fruit and flower bearers.

• If falling apples bother you, choose one of the ornamental crabs that keep their bright red fruits until winter when the birds eat them. These cultivars include 'Red Splendor', 'Prairie Fire', and 'Indian Magic'.

• Pear and apricot trees bloom beautifully and make nice, medium-sized shade trees. Although plum trees are not long-lived, they are small enough to be used in garden beds, breaking up monotonous vision lines. Some folks use them to add variety to long, narrow borders.

• My favorite small tree is the amur cherry *(Prunus maackii)*. Its orange bark is a real eye-catcher all year long. It doesn't have any messy fruits, and it shapes up nicely as it grows. It does not, however, like hot summer sun all day long. If you plant one, choose an area that will not have midday or hot afternoon sun.

• Another small and very showy tree for the garden is the Japanese tree lilac *(Syringa reticulata)*. Big, creamy white flowers appear in midsummer, providing cascades of white, flowing gracefully into the colored bloom of the garden.

• Pagoda dogwood *(Cornus alternifolia)* is a lovely small tree or large shrub that grows well in shade. Others that tolerate shade are serviceberry *(Amelanchier spp.)*, amur maple *(Acer ginnala)*, and *Magnolia x loebneri* 'Merrill'. If yours is a country life, maybe you can grow them all. Each one will become a very special focal point in your landscape.

Japanese tree lilac can be grown in either clump or tree form. (MSHS)

There are many other small trees, and almost every one will enhance either a small or a large yard. The only one that I don't appreciate is the Canada red chokecherry *(Prunus virginiana)*. Its appearance is not a problem, but it produces a lot of pesky suckers which pop out irritatingly all over the lawn.

Foundation Plantings

Fred Glasoe

I keep my camera handy in my car as I go about my daily errands in the Twin Cities area. I keep my eyes open for examples of good urban landscaping, but I take pictures of bad landscaping too. I try to obtain pictures of the average home, the average lot, and I frequently find old and overgrown plantings which have been in place for 20 or 30 years and are covering up both doors and windows. It's impossible to see the windows of many of these homes, and of course, the occupants cannot see out.

If yours is a home with the sidewalks partially blocked and doorways completely hidden, do some thinking. If junipers that were once planted in the open, hot sun are now thin and sickly from living under the deep shade of trees that were once potted saplings, consider what you might do. June and July are excellent times for replanting around your home.

Too often oversized shrubs are planted where they don't belong. Foundation plantings of French lilacs, sumacs, and other giant shrubs should never be planted where they will grow to cover doors and windows. One-story houses should never have plantings of "cover-up shrubs" or giant shade trees. As these grow, your home grows smaller by comparison. What used to look like a nice comfortable dwelling might end up looking like a Great Dane's doghouse.

Fifty-foot urban lots need dwarf or medium-sized shrubs, half-sized shade trees, and dwarf fruit trees. Each one of these can become a properly proportioned specimen which will draw admiration. Planting smaller shrubs and trees on small lots leaves room for needed garden sun and will surely help to create good lawn conditions.

If you are replacing foundation plantings, there are three possibilities. You can choose deciduous shrubs only, a mixture of evergreen and deciduous shrubs, or only evergreens. Don't underestimate the value of evergreens in our northern landscape plantings. In a climate which allows only six months of leaves on most trees and shrubs, evergreens are a necessity. Clumps of bare, colorless sticks rising out of snowdrifts in front of the house do not create an attractive image. Evergreens, both high and low-growing, will look good 12 months of the year and add color to an otherwise gray and white environment. For deciduous color, consider some dogwoods with their red or yellow twigs to color the snowy world.

Junipers, whether they are tall or creeping, must have good sun. If your junipers are shaded by mature trees, they could be candidates for replacement. Arborvitae will tolerate partial shade, but thrive best if they have half-day sun in the cool of the day. For sites with deep shade, the shrub of choice is the Cadillac of evergreens, the Japanese yew. Japanese yew are shade tolerant and can be bravely shaped and trimmed by those who like the formal English garden look. All of the evergreens come in both tall pyramid or upright shapes and low and medium-height spreading shapes. Most evergreens like acidic fertilizer. The exception is arborvitae, which likes regular, general plant food. Arborvitae likes to be moist, just like the yew family.

I don't want to give the impression that deciduous shrubs should be avoided. We can now purchase many beautiful, hardy flowering shrubs for our northern climate. Home landscapes are really being brightened by the 'Northern

Dwarf compact viburnum works well as a shrub border. (MSHS)

Lights' series of azaleas and the extremely hardy 'Northern Sun' forsythia. There are also red-flowered weigelas, the dwarf Korean and Chinese lilacs, yellow potentillas, red and white spireas, purple-leaved sand cherries, and light yellow-green mockorange shrubs. My favorite is the compact viburnum and the dwarf compact viburnum. These have dark, glossy green leaves that turn a deep burgundy in the fall. The bush keeps a nice compact form and is easy to shape.

Don't hesitate to look over the old homestead every so often, and if change is called for, be brave. Start anew.

For the Birds

Cynthia Lein

People install bird baths and feeders to attract birds to their yards, but there is an often overlooked, more natural approach. As wildlife habitats bow to the pressures of increased urbanization, richly diverse "homesteads" which provide all of a bird's needs are disappearing. While individual yards cannot erase the effects of development, residential landscapes can be planned with an eye toward increasing available nesting sites.

First, it is important to understand how birds select nesting sites. For many species this is the male's job. He builds one or more nests, even before a female has been attracted. The male's expertise at selecting an appropriate site has a great impact on how successful the family will be. What does he look for? Any good real estate agent can answer that: location, location, location.

Of course food is of primary importance. But, since feeding too close to the nest draws attention to the young, the food source should be a small distance away (even a few hundred feet is acceptable). There are many plants which pro-

The Nanking cherry is a broad, spreading shrub with fruits that birds love! (MSHS)

vide food for birds. Serviceberries *(Amelanchier* spp.) and Nanking cherries *(Prunus tomentosa)* have early ripening fruits which many birds enjoy. Oaks, willows, and birch trees support a great deal of insect life, which is just another form of bird food.

Water is another basic need. Insect-eaters, such as eastern kingbirds, prefer a lake or pond nearby, but other birds, such as chickadees and cardinals, will be content with a consistently filled birdbath.

Although tall trees are appreciated as singing posts, most birds prefer their nests to be between 5 and 15 feet off the ground. Trees and shrubs meeting this requirement will attract nesters. Branches should allow for easy escape, but be thick enough to make the nest inaccessible to cats and other predators—thorny plants are especially prized. Branches must be able to take the weight of the nest, remain stable in the wind, and have angles which will support the sides of the nest. Foliage acts as protection from sun and rain and provides concealment.

Existing plants can be maintained or modified to encourage nesting. Although wide-angled branches are usually recommended by pruning experts, leave some branches at a 70-degree angle to support nest sides. Birds prefer a site where three or more branches are growing close together. Preserve dead tree snags for cavity nesters, such as woodpeckers. By making your landscape more hospitable to birds, you'll be able to add their colors and textures to the design they inhabit.

Plants That Make Good Bird Homes

Look at your property from a bird's-eye view. How many prime

Spruce trees provide excellent winter cover for birds. (MSHS)

real estate listings do you see? If your property is sparsely planted or has only tall trees, consider adding some lower nesting sites. Diversity is critical. A wide variety of plant species and available nesting materials will increase the variety of birds that call your property home.

The following list shows a selection of trees and shrubs that make excellent nest sites or provide good winter cover:

Plants That Make Good Bird Homes

PLANTS	BIRDS ATTRACTED
EVERGREENS	
Canadian hemlock *Tsuga canadensis*	catbird, cardinal, purple finch, blue jay, mourning dove, robin, pine sisken
Arborvitae *Thuja occidentalis*	chickadee, nuthatch, purple finch, pine sisken, woodpecker
Spruce *Picea* spp.	chickadee, nuthatch, purple finch, pine sisken, woodpecker
DECIDUOUS TREES	
Cockspur hawthorn *Cratageus crusgalli*	robin, mourning dove, goldfinch, thrasher, thrush, warbler
Crab apple *Malus* spp.	robin, cardinal, goldfinch, flycatcher
Russian olive *Elaeagnus angustifolia*	robin, cardinal, thrasher, thrush
Apple, Pear *Malus* and *Pyrus* spp.	woodpecker, nuthatch, bluebird, wren, chickadee
DECIDUOUS SHRUBS	
Barberry *Berberis* spp.	warbler, catbird, vireo, cardinal, thrasher, thrush
Blueberry *Vaccinium* spp.	warbler
Elderberry *Sambucus* spp.	cardinal, thrush, thrasher
Lilac *Syringa* spp.	catbird, thrush, vireo

Landscaping for Wildlife

Mervin C. Eisel

Although man is crowding many of the native inhabitants off the land, this need not happen with birds which are very compatible and can add much interest to the landscape. However, they must be considered when developing and planting the land. Many bird food plants which can be selected for trees and shrub border provide habitat and food for the birds. Mass plantings are desirable for birds and often can be planted to reduce maintenance, thus giving the gardener more time to enjoy the birds.

Ornithologists estimate an acre of land in the eastern United States will support an average of four birds. By providing suitable habitat and plants that provide food during the winter months, this number can be increased considerably.

Four essentials for birds

A continuous supply of food is essential for all birds. Plants producing fruits and seed during the summer serve as a supplement to a bird's insect diet. Two of the best summer fruit trees for birds are the amur chokecherry and the black cherry.

Resident non-migratory birds also need fall food to build up food stores or fat reserves that allow them to survive the winter. Fruits of red-twigged dogwood, gray dogwood, mountain ash, winterberry, and buffaloberry are important foods for gray catbirds, brown thrashers, American robins, wood

Winterberry requires male and female plants to ensure fruiting. (MSHS)

thrushes, cedar waxwings, cardinals, purple finches, dark-eyed juncos, and black-capped chickadees. Also benefitting are white-breasted nuthatches, evening grosbeaks, ruffed grouse, bluebirds, and northern orioles.

Those plants that retain their fruits into the winter are especially important because food is scarce then. Examples of persistent foods are glossy black chokeberry, 'red splendor' crabapple, staghorn and smooth sumac, and American highbush cranberry. In addition to being a good food source, plants that retain their fruits into the winter often contribute color and interest to an otherwise drab win-

Fruits of the American highbush cranberry stay well into winter. (MSHS)

ter landscape.

Water must be available. A birdbath, a small pool, or fountain will fulfill this need. If possible, the water should be shallow, at least along the edge of the container. A supply of water can be maintained during the winter by using an electric bird-bath heater.

Birds must have protective cover. Cover helps them escape from cats, dogs, and natural predators and gives protection in bad weather. Dense evergreens effectively supply this protection. When landscaping especially to attract the birds, plants are spaced closer together than normal; therefore, thicket type planting is ideal, allowing the branches to grow close to the ground. Thicket-forming plants include chokecherry, black raspberry, red raspberry, blackberry, and serviceberry. This dense vegetative growth also will provide desirable nesting sites.

Birdhouses and feeders help attract birds to the landscape. Birdhouses should be protected from cats and squirrels. Should you desire to feed the birds during the winter, be sure to do so through the entire winter because birds become dependent on this food source.

The following charts list examples of trees and shrubs that attract birds. The season(s) when the birds use the plants for food is noted.

Trees

Amur Chokecherry: fall- winter; 20-30 ft.; nice winter interest with peeling bark becoming reddish-gray, shaggy, and peeling with age.

Black Clump Cherry: fall-winter; 20-30 ft.; good for bird sanctuaries.

Green Ash: fall-winter; 50 ft.

Mountain Ash: fall-winter; 30 ft.; pendant clusters of orange to scarlet fruits.

Hackberry: fall-winter; 50-60 ft.; extremely fast growing tree, similar to elm in looks.

Russian Olive: fall-winter; 20-25 ft.; flowers are small, yellow, and very fragrant.

Eastern Red Cedar 'Dundee': fall-winter; 12-18 ft.; good in sun or shade.

'Red Splendor' Crab: winter; 18 ft.; produces dark red fruit that is retained.

Cockspur Hawthorn: fall-winter; 15 ft.; species available without thorns.

'Meteor Cherry': summer; 10-12 ft.; bears attractive white flowers.

Tall Shrubs

Chokecherry: summer; 20 ft.; requires well-drained soil and sun.

Silver Buffaloberry: late summer; 10-13 ft.; silver foliage, bears orange-red fruit.

Shadblow Clump Serviceberry: summer; 20 ft.; fall color varies from yellow-gold to orange-red.

Amur Maple: fall-winter; 20-25 ft.; can be pruned to tree form, fast growing.

Allegany Clump Serviceberry: summer; 20-25 ft.; lovely white hanging flower clusters.

Nannyberry Viburnum: winter; 15-18 ft.; ideal for naturalizing borders and screening.

Medium Shrubs

Smooth Sumac: summer, fall, winter; 10 ft.; native shrub useful for tall bank cover, good in poor soil.

Staghorn Sumac: summer, fall, winter; 10 ft.; vivid orange to red fall color.

Gray Dogwood: summer; 8-10 ft.; easy to grow, hardy shrub, tolerates all soils, especially moist types.

Red-twig Dogwood: summer; 8-10 ft.; showy red stems, porcelain-blue fruit.

Winterberry: winter; 6-8 ft.; red berries Aug.-Sept., both sexes needed to insure fruiting.

Nanking Cherry: summer; 6-10 ft.; broad, spreading, dense shrubs with pink flowers in bud that open to white in early May.

Red Berried Elder: summer; 8-10 ft.; native shrub to Minnesota.

Adams Elder: summer; 8-10 ft.; use as background shrub, white flowers bloom in late June.

American Highbush Cranberry: winter; 7-12 ft.; leaves will turn bright red if plant is in sunny location.

Arrowwood Viburnum: summer-fall; 7-10 ft.; bears black fruit.

Dwarf Amur Maple: fall-winter; 6-8 ft.; dense, compact form of hardy shrub maple.

Short Shrubs

Raspberries: summer; 5 ft.; many varieties.

Blackberries: summer; 5 ft.; fruits ripen in July.

Blueberries: summer; 2 ft.; bright red leaves in fall.

Glossy Black Chokeberry: winter; 3-5 ft.; brilliant red fall color.

Gooseberries: summer; 4-6 ft.; shrubby bush fruit with some thorny spines.

Chart and article adapted from MN. Extension Service Bulletin No. 13-1972

Fall Color

Glenn Ray

Nothing captures the human eye like color. So it happens that autumn has become the season to celebrate trees. Waves of fall color usually begin to appear in mid-September in the far north and reach the southern part of Minnesota sometime in the middle of October.

These days of "peak autumn color" are the days when the red and sugar maples show their yellows, oranges, pinks, and scarlets. But there is more to northern autumn color than red and sugar maples, however spectacular they are. Following them are the yellows, reds, and wines of the native oaks and the yellows of the planted Norway maples. There are a good number of smaller trees coloring the landscape. Nor are the red and sugar maples the first to change. That distinction surely belongs to the staghorn sumac.

Autumn is a good time to plant trees for next year's fall color. The following list identifies expected fall colors and their peak times. Remember, many variables affect colors of autumn foliage, not the least of which is the genetic heritage of the individual tree and the nature of the environment where the tree is planted. Someone's white oak may become yellow, another's always wine red. In some seasons cottonwoods and Lombardy poplars show no autumn color change at all. And of course, each year's weather plays a major role.

The following chart lists the basic fall color sequence.

A mass of sumac adds a bold, early-fall color to your yard. (MSHS)

Fall Color Sequence

Early Season	Fall Color(s)
Staghorn sumac	orange, scarlet, purple
American basswood	yellow
Black walnut	yellow

Early Midseason	
Paper birch	yellow
Red maple	yellow, red, pink, orange
Sugar maple	yellow, orange, pink
Green ash	yellow
Mountain maple	yellow

Mid-season	
Winged euonymus	pink, rose, red
Quaking aspen	yellow
Korean mountain ash	orange
American mountain ash	orange, scarlet
European mountain ash	orange
Blue beech	orange, yellow, gold
Amur chokecherry	gold, orange
Cockspur hawthorn	gold, orange
River birch	yellow
Ironwood	yellow
Ohio buckeye	yellow, orange
Amur maple	yellow, orange, red

Late Midseason	
American elm	yellow
Silver maple	yellow, chartreuse
Eastern cottonwood	yellow
European larch	yellow, gold
American larch	yellow, gold
Honeylocust cultivars	yellow

Late season	
Norway maple	yellow
Schwedler maple	rust, orange
Amur corktree	yellow
Red oak	yellow, rust, orange, red, wine
White oak	yellow, rust, orange, wine
Ginkgo	yellow
Apricot	yellow
Lombardy poplar	yellow
Common buckthorn	yellow

Winter Interest

Glenn Ray

ouldn't you like your landscaping to be as attractive and interesting in mid-January as it is in mid-June? With the proper selection of trees and shrubs, it is very possible.

Winter gardens were often a topic for writers on landscape gardening during the early years of the century. Then for a time, planning for seasonal changes gave way to designing year-round patio and deck gardens, as the horticultural focus shifted from New England to California.

More recently, attention has refocused on winter landscapes and northern gardeners can glory in the opportunities that winter provides to create dramatically different effects. As a resident of Faribault, Minnesota, wrote in 1890: "The white tufts of snow perched upon the ten thousand green branches all about our dwelling transcends by far those calla lilies that we saw in California growing by the sea in January."

Snow—wondrous snow—is the element not to forget when planning a winter garden. Snow completely transforms the landscape, making it appear, as Mr. Baker wrote in 1914, "like another world, most wonderful and enchanting."

Winter gardens must be planned with snow in mind. Trees and shrubs which hold snow are prime plants for these gardens. Plants with interesting forms that show their silhouettes against the snow are also valuable. Color is always important, in winter as well as summer. Although plant colors are more subdued and less varied in winter, they can be very effective, especially when presented against a backdrop of snow. Premium plants for the winter garden, then, keeping the above elements in mind, are evergreen trees and shrubs and deciduous trees and shrubs with interesting form, texture, and color. The following list of plants contains those most often praised by winter landscape gardeners.

Evergreens Nearly all the northern evergreens are valuable for the winter garden, with the exception of those low-growing shrubs which would disappear beneath a foot or more of snow. Two evergreen trees should be singled out—the spruce, because of its magnificent form and its branches, which hold the snow superbly, and the Scot's pine because of its beautiful, cinnamon-colored bark.

Birch Valued for their interesting and colored bark, birch are especially effective when planted against a dark background. The white bark of the paper birch shows to good advantage against evergreens, while the river, cherry, and yellow birch all have colored bark.

Dogwoods These deciduous shrubs are highly valued for their colorful stems. Redosier dogwood

This paper birch stands out against a dark background. (MSHS)

(Cornus sericea) includes both red-twigged and yellow-twigged species.

Oaks The gnarled branches and impressive size of the oak tree give it a commanding presence in the winter landscape. Some oaks also retain their gold-brown leaves throughout winter.

Fruit-bearing shrubs Shrubs whose fruit hangs on through the winter, including winterberry *(Ilex verticillata)*, Korean barberry *(Berberis koreana)*, snowberry *(Symphoricarpos albus)*, American highbush cranberry *(Viburnum trilobum)*, and some flowering crabapple selections, such as 'Radiant' and 'Red Splendor', all add winter interest—as well as bird food.

Kentucky coffeetree *(Gymnocladus dioicus)* This tree has interesting bark and the added attraction of pods in winter.

Amur chokecherry *(Prunus maackii)* A small tree whose glossy reddish-brown bark tends to flake or peel like the native paper birch.

Chapter 5

Care and Maintenance

Successful Tree Planting

Protecting Trees and Shrubs

Pruning Mature Trees

Feeding the Trees

Successful Tree Planting

John Ball

Some homeowners believe that planting a tree is the easiest task in the world; just find a spot, dig a hole, and you're done! Nothing could be further from the truth. How carefully a tree is planted will set the stage for how it will grow in the years to come. Since a tree may live for many decades, isn't it worth a little extra effort to start the tree out right?

Buying the Tree

The planting process starts not with planting the tree, but with buying it. Starting with a healthy specimen can insure that your planting care will not be wasted. While at the garden center or nursery, look for trees with the following characteristics: normal shoot growth, no insect or disease problems, and no scars or torn bark. Also, note whether the garden center is storing the tree properly.

Regardless of which type of stock is purchased, whether bare root or balled and burlapped (B&B), the same storage care should be continued once the tree is home. Bare-root stock should have tree roots kept moist in a pail of damp chips or water, and the B&B stock should be kept with the burlap ball covered or hosed down and stored in the shade. If possible, the tree should be planted the day it is purchased. Even better, have the hole dug before you bring the tree home, and then plant immediately.

The Planting Hole

Where the hole is dug is very important. In addition to design considerations, homeowners often forget to check three critical items. First, see if the tree has enough room to reach its full height and spread. Always look up before planting, since power lines can cause problems in the years to come. Equally important, yet often neglected, is being certain the tree has enough area for the root system. Mature trees have a root system that extends far beyond the the crown. The ground within that area should be free of pavement or other barriers that impede the exchange of oxygen and carbon dioxide between soil and air.

Construction of the planting hole is as critical as its placement.

The hole should be dug no deeper than the depth of the roots, but the width should be several feet wider than the extent of the roots. This area of loose soil will allow more air space.

Fill the planting hole with the same soil you take out. Years ago, nurseries advised backfilling the planting hole with peat moss, composted manure, and rich top soil. This does not benefit the tree, however, and may even be detrimental to its survival. Abrupt changes of texture (soil particle size) has a great effect on moisture flow. If the backfill is coarser (larger particles such as sand) than the surrounding soil, water may not drain properly.

Some might think that if the soil is poor in their yard, providing a good backfill would help the tree get a good start. If the soil in the yard is that poor, however, perhaps the tree should not be planted; eventually its roots would grow out of the backfill. There are tree species that are native to wet sites, dry sites, and everything in between. Planting a tree that is naturally adapted to the soil in the area would be much wiser than modifying the planting soil to suit the tree.

Planting the Tree

Once the tree is set in the planting hole, be sure it is at the right depth. If it's too high, the roots may dry out; if it's too low, the roots may not receive enough oxygen. For B&B stock, the top of the ball should be at the soil surface. It's better to err in setting it slightly too high than too low, since the weight of the soil ball, especially with large trees, will cause some settling.

For bare-root trees, the depth of planting can be checked by looking at the bud union. Most ornamental trees are grafted, with the above-ground portion of the tree placed on the roots of another plant. At the base of the stem or trunk, there will be a small crook, where the top and roots meet. Place the crook an inch or two above the top of the planting hole.

When placing a bare-root tree in the hole, be sure not to twist any roots. The hole should be deep enough and wide enough to accommodate the roots without bending them. Twisting the roots to fit the hole may result in girdling of the roots as they increase in diameter, eventually resulting in crown die-back as the roots die. Once the roots are properly positioned, place soil around the roots until the hole is one-third filled, then add water. Once the ground has settled, fill another third and repeat the process until the hole is filled. Be sure to complete this entire process as quickly as possible, since the roots that are not covered are prone to drying.

For B&B stock, the same process is followed. Since the root system is enclosed in a burlap ball, there is no need to worry about twisting the roots. The burlap need not be removed; generally it will disintegrate within six months to a year. Plastic wrapping, however, should be carefully cut away and removed; plastic may take years to break down, and during that time, it will restrict root development. Just before the hole is completely filled in, cut away any twine wrapped around the base of the trunk.

Care of the New Tree

With either type of planting material, bare root or B&B, the planting is not finished when the tree is in the ground. Other tasks remain. Be sure to keep a grass-free area (with a radius of at least a foot, more if possible) around the tree. Grass is tough competition for young trees, and they will recover from transplant shock much more quickly if their competition is reduced. This grass-free strip can be left bare, or even better, covered with mulch. A mulch will keep the root area cool and moist. The best mulch is a two or three-inch layer of composted wood chips; a deeper mulch may prevent oxygen from penetrating the soil, while a shallower mulch may not provide any benefit. Composted chips should be used, since fresh chips may have bacteria and draw nitrogen from the soil as they break down.

After planting, a portion of the tree crown is sometimes pruned away, in the belief that because the root area is reduced, the crown must also be reduced. For many species, however, the spring root growth is triggered by the stem's expanding terminal buds, which release a chemical that initiates root growth. If these buds are removed, root growth may be delayed. During the first year after planting, therefore, pruning should be limited to removing broken, diseased, or poorly positioned branches.

Another common practice is staking newly planted trees. Approach this practice, however, with a great deal of caution. Improper staking, or stakes left on too long, are among major reasons for tree mortality. Unstaked trees generally develop a better taper and root system than their staked counterparts. Do not stake unless the tree cannot stand against the wind without support. If staking is required, one 2 x 2-inch stake should be driven in the ground about one foot from the trunk. Attach a single tie at about two-thirds the height of the tree and tie it to the stake. The tie should be elastic webbing to provide some movement and reduce bark damage. When the tree is staked, it should still be able to move several inches in response to the force of the wind. Also, be sure to remove the stake within a year of planting to prevent girdling at the tie.

There is some question as to whether newly transplanted trees should be fertilized. While most studies have found no harm fertilizing at transplant time, few have discovered any benefit. Apparently, trees have to recover from transplant shock before fertilizers are useful. This is not true of watering, however. Be sure to water the tree for the first two years after transplanting. New trees can use about one inch of water per week.

If all these steps are followed — proper selection of species and site, carefully constructed planting hole, placement of the tree, and good care after transplanting — the tree will be off to a good start at its new location. The few hours spent carefully following the planting procedure will return a lifetime of beauty and cooling shade.

After-Care Checklist

- ☐ Water is the critical factor for tree survival after planting. Deep water regularly throughout the first growing season. Allow water to run slowly, soaking the soil, once or twice a week. Do not over water.
- ☐ Keep lawn mowers and string trimmers away from tree to avoid wounding trunk.
- ☐ Reduce herbicide use near tree and in surrounding lawn.
- ☐ Never fertilize stressed trees. Fertilizer is not tree food. It should be applied only after first year if required.
- ☐ Replace mulch as needed. Keep grass and weeds out of mulched area. They compete for the same water and elements as tree.
- ☐ Remove stakes and strapping after one year unless site is extremely windy. Do not stake longer than 2 years.
- ☐ Prune dead or injured branches immediately.
- ☐ Prune while young to maintain size and shape beginning in the second growing season.
- ☐ Do not top trees to reduce height.
- ☐ Do not plant flowers under a tree. Do not cultivate soil under the tree.

Protecting Trees and Shrubs Against Winter Damage

Minnesota's harsh climate is responsible for a lot of damage to plants in the landscape. Winter sun, wind, and cold temperatures can burn evergreens, damage bark and kill branches, flowerbuds, and roots, while snow and ice can break branches and topple entire trees. Salt used for deicing pavements is harmful to landscape plantings. Winter food shortages force rodents and deer to feed on bark, twigs, and foliage injuring and sometimes killing trees and shrubs. All is not bleak, however, for there are some things we can do to protect our landscape plants and help minimize any injury.

Cold Damage

Cold temperatures can cause damage in several ways. Plants that are not hardy in Minnesota will be killed by early frost or low temperatures, but plants that normally grow here may be injured as well.

Sun Scald

Sun scald is characterized by elongated, sunken, dried or cracked areas of dead bark, usually on the south or southwest side of a tree. On a cold winter day, the sun can heat up bark to the point where cellular activity begins. When the sun goes behind a cloud or building, the bark temperature drops rapidly, killing the active tissue.

Young trees, newly planted trees, and thin barked trees (cherry, crabapple, honeylocust, linden, maple, mountain ash, and plum) are most susceptible to sun scald. Trees that have been heavily pruned or transplanted from a shady to a sunny area are also sensitive because of the loss of shading from other branches. Older trees are less subject to sun scald because the thicker bark can insulate the dormant tissue from the sun's heat.

Sun scald can be prevented by wrapping the trunk with a commercial tree wrap paper, plastic tree guards, or any other light colored material. The wrap will reflect the sun and keep the bark at a more constant temperature. Put the wrap on in the fall and remove it in the spring after the last frost. Newly planted trees should be wrapped for at least 2 winters and thin barked species up to 5 winters or more.

To repair sun scald damage, cut the dead bark back to live tissue with a sharp knife, forming the wound in the general shape of an elipse with rounded ends to facilitate healing. Wrap the trunk in subsequent winters to prevent further damage.

Winter Browning of Evergreens

Browning of evergreen foliage occurs when winter sun and wind cause excessive transpiration (foliage water loss) while the roots in frozen soil are unable to replace lost water. Browning, like sun scald, can also be caused by rapid drops in foliage temperature resulting when the sun drops out of sight on a cold winter day. Damage normally occurs on the south, southwest, and windward side of the plant, but in severe cases the whole plant may be affected. Yew, arborvitae, and hemlock are the most susceptible, but winter browning can affect all evergreens. New transplants are particularly sensitive. There are several ways to minimize winter browning damage. The first is proper placement of evergreens in the landscape. Yew, hemlock, and arborvitae should not be planted on south or southwest sides of buildings or in highly exposed places. A second way to reduce damage is to prop pine boughs or Christmas tree greens against or over evergreens to protect them from wind and sun and to catch more snow for natural cover.

Winter browning can be prevented by constructing a barrier of burlap or similar material on the south, west, and windward sides of the evergreen. If a plant has been showing injury on all sides, surround it with a barrier, but leave the top open to allow for some air and light penetration. Keeping evergreens well watered throughout the growing season and into the fall is another way to reduce winter burn. Watering only in the late fall does not help reduce injury.

Anti-desiccant and anti-transpirant sprays are often recommended to prevent winter burn. Most studies, however, have not shown them to be effective and in some cases there has been more damage with them than without them.

If an evergreen has suffered winter burn, wait until late spring before doing any repair. The brown foliage is dead and will not green up, but the buds, which are more protected than the foliage, will often grow out and cover up the brown. If the buds have not survived, prune off the dead branches, and fertilize in early spring. You should water the tree well throughout the season and provide some protection the following winter.

Die Back

Deciduous trees and shrubs can suffer from winter shoot die back and bud death. Flower buds are the most susceptible to injury. A good example of this is forsythia, which grows well, but often flowers very poorly.

There is little you can do to protect trees and shrubs from winter die back. Plants that are not completely hardy should be planted in a sheltered location. Plants in a vigorous growing condition late in the fall are more likely to suffer winter die back, so avoid late summer pruning and fertilizing. Apply fertilizer in the spring or in the fall after the leaves have dropped.

Root Injury

Roots do not become dormant in the winter as do the stem, branches, and buds and so they are less hardy than the tops. The roots of most trees and shrubs that grow in this state will be killed at temperatures below 0° to +10°F. These plants survive in Minnesota because the soil temperature normally is much higher than the air temperature.

Many things influence soil temperature. Moist soil holds more heat than dry, so in a sandy soil or during a dry year, frost penetration will be deeper and soil temperatures colder. Snow cover acts as an insulator, as does mulch, keeping the soil temperature higher. With newly planted trees, any cracks in the planting hole will allow the cold air to penetrate into the root zone.

To reduce root kill, mulch new trees and shrubs with 4 to 6 inches of a material, such as wood chips or straw if snow cover is unreliable. If the fall has been dry, water heavily before the ground freezes to reduce frost penetration. Check new plantings for cracks in the planting holes and fill them with soil. Check stakes and guy wires to be sure they are tight to prevent further cracking.

Heaving

Repeated freezing and thawing in the spring causes soil to expand and contract which can result in heaving shrubs and new plantings out of the ground. A 2 to 6-inch layer of mulch will prevent heaving by maintaining a more constant soil temperature.

Ice and Snow Damage

Heavy snow and ice storms cause damage by bending and breaking branches. Multiple leader upright evergreens, such as arborvitae and juniper, and multiple leader or clump trees, such as birch, are most subject to damage. Relatively small trees can be wrapped together with heavy twine or the leaders tied with strips of carpet, strong cloth, or nylon stockings two-thirds of the way above the crotch. These wrappings must be removed in the spring to prevent girdling and allow free movement of the stem. For trees with large, widespreading branches or large, multistemmed trees, the branches should be cabled together by a professional arborist.

Salt Damage

Salt used for deicing roads in the winter can cause or aggravate winter burn and die back. In addition, salt runoff can injure roots and be absorbed by the plant, ultimately damaging the foliage.

To prevent salt damage, do not plant trees and shrubs where salt is present. Avoid areas where salty runoff collects and where salt spray kicked up by cars may land on plants. Burlap barriers will protect plants from salt spray.

Animal Damage

Mice, rabbits, and deer are the main culprits causing damage in the winter. These animals feed on the tender twigs and foliage of landscape plants. They can girdle trees or eat shrubs to the ground line.

Rodents

Trees can be protected from rodent damage by placing a cylinder of 1/4-inch mesh hardware cloth around the trunk. The cylinder should extend 2 to 3 inches below the ground line for mice and 18 to 24 inches above the anticipated snow line for rabbit protection. The hardware cloth can be left on year around, but it should be larger than the trunk to allow for growth. For small trees, plastic tree guards are also effective. You can protect shrub beds from rabbits by fencing the beds with chicken wire.

If you have many trees or shrubs to protect, using screens may be too expensive and time consuming. In such a situation, repellents may be the best solution. Remember that a repellent is not a poison; it simply renders the plant undesirable through taste or smell.

Deer

Deer feed on and damage tops and side branches of small trees and shrubs. Repellents containing thiram give effective control. For deer exclosures to be effective, fences must be high and constructed with posts and heavy wire mesh. However, this is usually not feasible. If deer are starving, there is little you can do to prevent feeding. Providing a more palatable forage may help, but it may also attract more deer.

This article was reprinted from the 6th Edition of the Forest management Digest and is a Minnesota Extension Service bulletin.

Pruning Mature Trees

Tom Prosser

roper pruning of large shade trees is important to the health of a tree and will greatly extend its life. However, pruning is not a simple task and is often done incorrectly, leaving the tree stressed rather than revitalized. The pruning of a mature tree should be determined by the tree species, its size, and its current growth patterns. Every time a branch is removed there should be a good reason for it, based on an overall plan for the tree.

A well-pruned tree is a safer tree. With correct thinning, wind will blow through the tree instead of up against it and help reduce limb breakage in storms. Also, removing dead, diseased, and weak branches will insure that they do not fall on property or people.

Understanding how trees respond to pruning in general, as well as how individual species respond,will insure that the job is done the right way. Here are a few guidelines that should always be followed when pruning mature trees.

• Never prune branches in the middle or leave stubbed ends. This is known as topping, heading back, or pollarding. This practice is very damaging to a tree and will greatly reduce its life. A branch pruned in the middle has no defense against decay, and often a decay pocket will form at the cut and spread down the inside of the branch. A branch cut in the middle will grow increasingly weaker. Often a large tree that was previously topped will drop large branches for no apparent reason, even on a calm day. People who think they are making a tree safer by topping to reduce its height have actually made the tree more unsafe. If a branch needs to be cleared away from a house, power lines, or other obstacles, it should be removed back to the trunk or to another main limb.

• Topping trees has other negative side effects. It removes the terminal growth on the tree. This shocks the tree and induces it to grow large amounts of suckers. These suckers are weaker than the original terminal growth. Because of the large volume of suckers that are produced, the branches will become top-heavy and very thick within a few years. Combine this with the introduction of decay, and it can produce a very dangerous situation.

• Remove several small branches instead of a few large limbs. Removing smaller limbs reduces the amount of foliage taken out of a tree and keeps the tree's shape intact. If too many large limbs are removed, it will stress the tree and excessive sucker growth will result. Pruning should not produce large gaps in the tree. In a mature tree these gaps will never fill in.

• Cut living and dying branches as close as possible to the branch collar (see drawing). The branch collar should never be removed nor should stubs be left on the tree. The collar is very important tree tissue; it contains disease-fighting substances and prevents decay-causing organisms from entering the tree. Removing the collar can lead to serious problems. Here is how you prune specific trees:

Paper Birch

Remove only dead, dying, or rubbing limbs. Paper birches should seldom be thinned—thinning a birch will rob it of the protective cooling the branches provide in summer, weakening the tree and causing excessive dehydration. Because birch trees are usually stressed in normal landscape environments, they need all the leaves they can get to manufacture food. With the onslaught of the bronze birch borer in recent years, many birch trees have died. This insect will only attack a weak

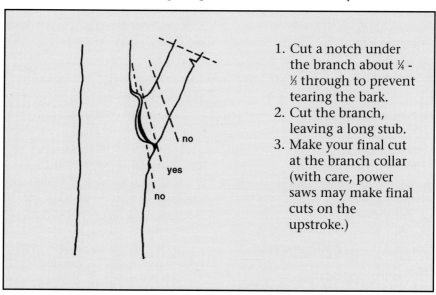

1. Cut a notch under the branch about ¼ - ⅓ through to prevent tearing the bark.
2. Cut the branch, leaving a long stub.
3. Make your final cut at the branch collar (with care, power saws may make final cuts on the upstroke.)

tree, making it even more important to be careful when pruning. If pruning is required, paper birch can be safely pruned from August 1 to April 1.

American Elm, Silver Maple, and Green Ash

These three trees grow very quickly and usually need to be thinned quite a bit, as well as have their deadwood removed. When pruning these trees, thin the ends of each branch and remove a large number of small limbs rather than a few large limbs. As a general rule, one-fourth to one-third of the crown of these trees can be taken out without changing the shape of the tree. It is very common to see these trees pruned halfway out on each branch. This does very little for the tree and will leave a branch with lots of smaller branches out on the end and nothing in the middle. A pole saw is an effective way to thoroughly prune at the ends of each branch.

Elms should only be pruned after the first hard frost of autumn until April 1 because of Dutch elm disease. Silver maple and green ash can be pruned anytime during the year.

Sugar and Norway Maple

Because of the slow growth rate of these trees, they rarely need to be thinned. If they are thinned too often they begin to decline in vigor. However, deadwood should be periodically pruned out to remove decay organisms and allow the tree to seal. Topping will usually kill these trees. Both can be pruned at anytime during the year.

Bur and White Oaks

These trees also have a slow rate of growth and should be only lightly thinned, if at all. It is important to periodically remove deadwood. These trees often have suckers growing on the trunks or at the base of large branches. These are not harmful to the tree and can either be left on or removed, depending on the look the homeowner prefers. If removed, these sucker branches will immediately start to grow back.

Bur and white oak should not be pruned between April 15 and July 1, to avoid oak wilt disease.

Red Oak

This tree has a medium growth rate and is highly variable in how it should be pruned. If growing outside a wooded situation, the red oak can become very thick and will need to be thinned. Red oaks have a highly complex branching system that produces hundreds of small twigs at the ends of the branches. This makes it very important to do most of the thinning at the ends of the branches, not necessarily pruning twigs, but rather thinning out the branches producing the twigs.

Red oaks usually contain above average amounts of decay and are often hollow, making it important to keep deadwood out of the tree and to keep an eye on potential structural problems. A red oak with sharp-angled major limbs should have support cables installed to prevent breakage.

Red oaks should not be pruned between April 15 and July 1 to avoid oak wilt.

Fruit Trees

Fruit trees should periodically be lightly thinned and have deadwood removed. Trees that are over-trimmed will produce weak and disease-susceptible sucker growth. If a tree needs heavier thinning, do it in stages over a period of three years. Sucker branches can be removed and the wound treated with a substance that contains a growth inhibitor. On large trees, avoid removing live limbs over four inches in diameter, as this will also induce sucker growth. Removing large limbs on mature trees may leave wounds that never heal. The result can be decay entering the tree, causing dieback on the trunk.

A young fruit tree should be pruned within two years of planting to establish the future strength of its structure. Fruits trees should

be pruned only when temperature is below 32°F, to prevent infection by fire blight.

Pine and Spruce Trees

These trees are very different from deciduous trees—they should not be thinned. If they have dead-wood, they are probably sick. If left untreated, the disease will continue to progress until the tree is either dead or too unsightly to keep. When treating a diseased pine or spruce it is a good idea to remove the infected limbs to eliminate as much of the disease as possible. If these trees are planted too close together, they will die out on the sides that are up against each other, because not enough sunlight reaches those limbs.

Never cut off the leader of these trees. Whenever you cut off the top of a pine or spruce, two new leaders will grow in place of the first one, throwing off the shape of the tree. Pruning diseased limbs on pines or spruces should only be done during dry weather.

Feeding the Trees

Dave Swanson

Any tree, young or old, is a candidate for fertilization. The additional nutrients cause the leaves to grow larger and darker, increase root growth, and improve overall vigor, making trees less susceptible to most pests and diseases. Even trees in declining health can sometimes recover with timely fertilizer applications.

The three main nutrients for trees, like most other plants, are nitrogen, phosphorus, and potassium. Here are the four basic methods of tree fertilization, each with its advantages and disadvantages:

Broadcast surface application—simply sprinkling the fertilizer on the ground under the tree—is an easy method and effective for applying nitrogen. Phosphorus and potassium, which do not move readily into and through the soil, should not be applied in this manner. For trees surrounded by turf, broadcast applications are best made in late fall after the turf goes dormant.

Soil incorporation places nutrients directly into the root zone and makes them readily available for the tree. Liquid fertilizers can be injected directly into the ground, or granular fertilizer can be placed in holes drilled into the ground. The holes will increase aeration and water penetration to the roots. This method requires special equipment, such as a high-pressure pump or soil auger.

Foliar sprays are useful for quickly overcoming nutrient deficiency symptoms, such as iron chlorosis. To maintain its effectiveness, spraying needs to be repeated frequently and may leave a whitish film or spots on the leaves.

Trunk injections are used on particular "problem trees" where other methods are inefficient or inappropriate. Injection can be effective in correcting micronutrient deficiencies, although some decay may occur around the injection sites.

Tree fertilization is a procedure that encourages rapid development and continuing good health. A professional arborist can be helpful in recommending the proper nutrients, method, and timing for your trees.

Gardening Skill

Fertilizing Trees and Shrubs: Amount to Apply

Most trees in the northern states and Canada have a single flush of growth in the spring. This is when the plants have the greatest need for nutrients. A fall application of fertilizer is the easiest and probably the most effective because the ground is easier to work and the nutrients will be available very early in the spring when growth begins. The following chart lists the application amounts for a basic 10-10-10 mix. Remember, these quantities of fertilizer cannot be applied to turf.

Diameter of Spread	Sq. Ft. Area	Amount/year 10-10-10
1 Ft.	1.5	1.5 tbl.
2	3.1	3 tbl.
3	7	7 tbl.
4	12.5	¾ cups
5	20	1¼ cups
6	28	1¾ cups
7	38	2¼ cups
8	50	3½ cups
9	64	4¼ cups
10	78	5 cups
15	177	12 cups
20	314	21½ cups (9 lbs.)
25	490	33 cups (14.5 lbs.)
30	706	21 pounds

USDA Plant Hardiness Zone Map

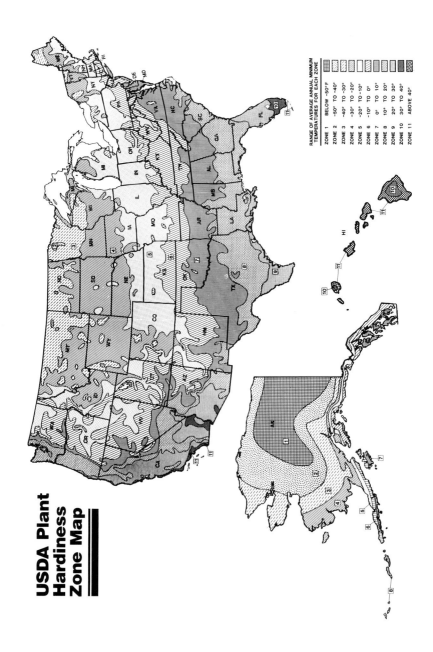

RANGE OF AVERAGE ANNUAL MINIMUM
TEMPERATURES FOR EACH ZONE

ZONE 1	BELOW -50°F
ZONE 2	-50° TO -40°
ZONE 3	-40° TO -30°
ZONE 4	-30° TO -20°
ZONE 5	-20° TO -10°
ZONE 6	-10° TO 0°
ZONE 7	0° TO 10°
ZONE 8	10° TO 20°
ZONE 9	20° TO 30°
ZONE 10	30° TO 40°
ZONE 11	ABOVE 40°

About the Authors

John Ball has a PhD in Urban Forestry and currently works at South Dakota State University. In addition to teaching horticulture in South Dakota, Michigan, and Minnesota, John owned a commercial tree service in Duluth, Minnesota.

Fred Glasoe, Minneapolis, Minnesota, has been a regular contributor to *Minnesota Horticulturist* since 1972 and hosts a weekly radio program on gardening. An avid promoter of gardening in the North, Fred is Past President of MSHS and a life-time member of the organization.

Carroll L. Henderson works for the Minnesota Department of Natural Resources and is author of the book *Landscaping for Wildlife*.

Kate Hintz is an avid gardener who shares her gardening experiences from Mahtomedi, Minnesota. She is a member of the Washington County Horticultural Society.

Dorothy Johnson is Executive Director of MSHS. As a volunteer in horticulture, she has been a Master Gardener since 1977 and is active in local and regional garden organizations.

Paul B. Kannowski, from Grand Forks, North Dakota, is a professor at the University of North Dakota. He authored *Wildflowers of North Dakota*.

Cynthia Lein volunteers at the Raptor Center at the University of Minnesota, St. Paul, and combines her interest of wildlife with gardening.

Jane P. McKinnon Extension Horticulturist (retired) University of MN.

Tom Prosser is a tree care specialist with a business headquartered in St. Louis Park, Minnesota.

Glenn Ray was Executive Secretary of MSHS for several years. He presently owns a garden design service.

Peggy Sand is a registered landscape architect and lecturer at the University of MN. Department of Landscape Architecture.

Terry Schwartz, a native of northern Minnesota, now lives in Cottage Grove. He is employed by a large wholesale nursery, with growing ranges in Minnesota, Oregon, and Washington.

Dave Swanson is a tree care professional working in the Minneapolis - St. Paul area.

Katherine Widin is a plant pathologist, who is employed as a City Forester and maintains a horticultural consulting firm in Stillwater, Minnesota.